PEOPLE DO CHANGE

1"Edition

ISBN-13: 978-1985567023

ISBN-10: 1985567024

This assumption by the subject of his history,
insofar as is constituted by speech addressed to another,
is clearly the basis of the new method Freud called psychoanalysis.
— Jacques Lacan

He who hopes to learn the fine art of the game of chess from books
will soon discover that only the opening and closing moves of
the game admit of exhaustive systematic description, and that
the endless variety of the moves which develop
from the opening defies description.
— Sigmund Freud

TABLE OF CONTENTS

I.	What is Psychotherapy?	7
II.	Make Room for Death	29
III.	The Betrayal of Cats	37
IV.	The Freedom of Not Eating	43
V.	Make the Time: How do you deal with an exhausting workload?	51
VI.	A Loneliness that Entangles	59
VII.	When Passion Ends	69
VIII.	Infidelity as a Trauma	81
IX.	Raising a Teenager	93
X.	Children's drawings as a message to the parents	101
XI.	How to Deal with Madness?	107
XII.	The Moment of Concluding	115

I. WHAT IS PSYCHOTHERAPY?

"People don't change." How many times have you heard that statement? How many times have you said it? It's a firm belief for a lot of people, one that frequently comes out of our lips when we stop trusting in someone, decide to not give another chance to those who have disappointed us, or even to excuse ourselves from a mistake that we make over and over again.

An important part of being a psychotherapist is believing that, in different ways, people do change. Even though the enormous difficulty of change is recognized in most psychological theories, with each theory espousing different causes for the difficulty, they all agree that people do change.

But to what kind of change am I referring in this book? If I were talking about a change in respect to an illness with a biological cause, it would be easy to explain: the change we seek would be for the patient to be free of the disease or physical disorder. When it comes to mental illness, it is not so straightforward. For that, first we would have to be clear about what illness or problem are we facing.

A common example of biological illness would be a pathology that causes fever. Let's think of Mary, a forty year old woman who discovers she has a temperature of 39C (102F) and decides to go to her doctor. The physician measures her temperature with a thermometer, maybe a bit more sophisticated than the one she has at home, and they confirm it's higher than 39C while also observing the typical sweating that accompanies a fever.

What do we do when someone has a fever? What does a doctor do? Unless it's a very severe case, they don't intervene directly in the high temperature (i.e. submerging the patient in a cold bath), but instead try to find the cause of the fever and act upon it with a specific medication such as antibiotics given to treat a fever caused by an infection.

Fever
_____

Infection (cause of the fever) ← Intervention

Let's think now of an analogous situation in a psychotherapist's case. A person can go to a psychoanalyst practice, a mental health center, or even a psychiatric ward with thousands of different issues. Let's take the case of Emily, a sixty year old woman that arrives at my office stating *"I came because I am depressed."* A clear statement detailing a specific concern of the client, but a much more complicated beginning for the treating professional than our fever example.

When our first example patient, Mary, went to her physician because of her fever, she introduces herself explaining she is worried about her high temperature. She could even have said nothing, allowing her doctor to examine her first, and it would be fair to assume they would have quickly detected the high fever through direct observation and routine diagnostic testing. This process is fairly straight forward and procedural in nature, the doctor is able to identify and confirm the illness quickly and efficiently in most cases.

What is observable and measurable when a patient arrives at the office of a psychotherapist? The initial material with which a therapist can engage is what the patient says, how they present their story, and their discourse with the therapist.

Confronted by Mary's statement about her temperature, the doctor would first use his own thermometer to verify it. But confronted with a word, with a simple statement such as *"I am depressed"*, what 'thermometer' would we use? What instrument is useful for this? As psychotherapists our instrument is listening. Later on in this chapter I will explain how, in psychoanalysis, we will use a particular way of listening but, even in its more common definition, listening is the instrument needed to begin to explore what the patient brings to our office.

But since anyone can listen to Emily say the words *"I am depressed"*, it can't be the mere possibility of hearing that statement that defines our work. If that would be the case, any conversation would be the equivalent of psychotherapy. Is it to be able to effectively determine if she is indeed depressed that defines our work? To know if she is using the term correctly? To be able to discern if the necessary criteria to diagnose depression are met in this case?

Those questions may be relevant to a psychiatrist -or to a psychotherapist whose practice is deeply rooted in the psychiatric logic of the Diagnostic and Statistical Manual of Mental Disorders (a directory of specific disorders, their diagnostic criteria and etiology, commonly referred to as the

DSM and widely held to be the universal compendium defining mental illnesses and disorders). This type of definition is important for a psychiatrist because, like the doctor treating Mary's fever, their treatment modality focuses on what medication is required to treat the patient, and therefore a diagnosis of a specific disorder is needed.

The interesting thing is that —at least temporarily— questions about 'accurate' diagnosis are not relevant in a psychotherapeutic setting. In contrast to medicine, to the majority of psychotherapists it's not relevant to know if all the criteria of depression are met, or if what the patient refers to as 'depression' is really something called by another term in our profession. The term that the patient uses to name their suffering serves as an introduction and an explanation as to why they have requested our services, but it's not the key of our intervention since it is not what will allow a change in them.

What is the key then? As with a fever that is not usually treated directly by addressing only the temperature itself, psychotherapists are not going to intervene in what is perceptible, the statement *"I am depressed"*. Instead, we would focus on what causes that statement to appear.

Thus, we find ourselves in the field of subjectivity. The cause that we search for is not the obvious one, the direct cause, in other words. In Emily's example, she could say she is depressed because her husband passed away. But the death of her husband is not the cause of the depression. After all, we could imagine certain situations in which some people may feel happy for the passing of their partner.

In this case, the death of her husband has caused distress because Emily was certain that she would not be able to live without him. That belief existed in a gap between the objective fact, the death of her husband, and her feeling depressed. It's exactly there, in that gap, where we found Emily's subjectivity, or even herself as a subject, and it's there where we found why she is depressed.

$$\frac{\text{I am depressed}}{\frac{\text{I can't live without him} \leftarrow \text{Subjective Position}}{\text{Husband's death}}}$$

In the words of Jacques Lacan "what is certain is that the symptom will only give in to an intervention interceding at the decentred level."[1] It is there where we will intervene, exploring that feeling, examining and questioning that belief, analyzing what her husband meant to her, and other approaches dependent on the individual patient. And as this treatment unfolded, over a couple of months, it allowed Emily to, indeed, continue her life without her husband.

It is this position in relation to her experience that a person can change. Emily will still be Emily and her husband will still be dead, but she will no longer believe she is not able to live without him. Once she stops believing that, there is no doubt her future will be different.

When utilizing our instrument, that of listening, we strive to listen on two different levels. The first level being what is said, that is the statement itself, and the second being the place from where those statements are uttered. The statement is what we can hear or read when a person is talking or writing, the material aspect of it. The subjective position that we try to find refers to that virtual place from which they are speaking. In Emily's example, the statement *"I am depressed"* is said from a place ruled by a discourse that supports her depression, for example, *"I am not able to live without the man with whom I have made all the important decisions of my life, especially in my old age and without a close relationship to my children."*

It is not necessary for the subjective position to be put in words like that; most of the time it's just a synthesis made by the psychotherapists to themselves, to be able to better understand the case. What is important is that it would be in this in-between space where the intervention will be applied, between the fact and the effect it has on the patient, and not directly upon the patient's statements.

> I am depressed
> _____
> I can't live without him ← Subjective Position ← Intervention
> Husband's death

In summary, it seems that what defines the psychotherapeutic practice is the searching and intervening within the place from where the statements are said, that gap where the subjectivity resides, more than intervening in the statement itself. Through these interventions we try to produce the desired change in the life of the person, thanks to the change in their subjective position that ultimately determines their experience.

It is important to clarify that there is consensus in the psychotherapeutic schools in regards to considering that the patient communicates with us not only through verbal communication; everything they do and do not do is communication and we take into consideration even what they say without knowing they are speaking, like Lacan postulates in 1953: "Even through his body, the subject emits a speech, which is, as such, speech of truth, a signifying speech which he does not even know he emits. It is because he always says more than he means to, always more than he thinks he says."[2]

Through what the patient says to us —verbally and non-verbally— we try to find the place from which they are talking, as this reveals a great deal about their experiences and perspectives. In doing so we ensure that what they say is put into their personal context, their history, family, and culture. That may seem obvious, but it's not always clear in the treatment given by some psychotherapists.

Lacan gave us an example of a patient he saw who had trouble using his hand. The man had been treated by another psychoanalyst before, who had focused their interpretations on his masturbation and its repression by the environment. That hypothesis only builds on the well-known caricature that for psychoanalysis everything is about sex.

Lacan, on the other hand, listened to the history of the subject, whose family of origin was Muslim. The key was to stick to his precept that "one should not fail to recognize the symbolic surroundings of a subject."[3] Like some of you know, in the law of the Koran the punishment for a thief is to have their hand cut off. Even if that punishment is not enforced now, it's still inscribed in the symbolic order that serves as a foundation for human relationships. The patient had learned in his childhood that his father had lost his job for being accused of robbery. If the patient had troubles using his hand, it was not by some repressed childhood masturbation, but for an identification with his father who, according to the Koran, should have lost his hand.

In this example we can see why the place where we live, our traditions and family history, indeed all the levels of our personal context, are key to understanding what we say and what is happening to us. Psychotherapy will only work when their interventions take all of that into account.

Another example is a simple, harmless seeming, statement like *"I am smart."* Even if it can sound harmless or even positive, it could also become problematic if the person seems unable to occupy the place that their statement creates as their identity. This is something that happens to a lot of high school students with excellent grades, that once at the university level they become average. Is their definition of intelligence the problem? Did they cease to be smart? Were they actually smart before? Part of psychotherapy will be to put all of that into question, not to discover whether or not they are smart by following an objective criterion, but to explore the subjective position that produces suffering in this person, in their particular situation, because of their choice of defining themselves as smart.

The key to generate a change in our patients is to shift the subjective position of the individual, the position from which they observe and live their own experience. Sounds easy?

One of the first problems to achieve this change is that people are not necessarily aware of their own position.

How can we ignore what defines us, that position from which we experience life? There are different theories that explain this, but in this book I will use two thinkers from different fields of study who both highlight this fact: the marketing research done by Howard Moskowitz, and the psychoanalytic theory created by Sigmund Freud.

I heard this story for the first time on Malcolm Gladwell's famous TED talk. Prego, the tomato sauce company, hired Moskowitz's consulting company to help them beat their competition. What did Moskowitz do? He made almost fifty varieties of tomato sauce, rating them according to different factors such as sweetness, garlic content, acidity, and spice, among others.

Once his sauces were ready, he toured the United States, asking thousands of people to taste them. Each person was served ten tiny plates of pasta, with a different sauce in each, and they were asked to score them.

When he analyzed the data he didn't look for the most popular variety of sauce -what other marketing experts of the time would have done. Instead, he grouped the results in a way that showed that every American belongs to one of three groups. One third of them like their tomato sauce normal, another third like it spicy, and the last third like it extra chunky.

Therein lay the key to Prego, since at that time there was no chunky tomato sauce on the market. They took control of the market with that variety, earning more than six hundred million dollars with it in the following years.

What does tomato sauce have to do with psychotherapy? Before Moskowitz, what marketing research did to find out what people wanted was simply asking them. For years they sat people down in focus groups and asked them directly: *"How do you like your tomato sauce?"* During all that time, more than thirty years, no one said they liked it chunky. Even when for a third of them, that's what they actually liked.

What I'm trying to show with this brief story is that our own desires —even the most simple ones— are not transparent to ourselves. The position from where we observe our lives and ourselves, the possibility and capacity to know ourselves, is not as clear and already accessible as we want to believe because it is framed and limited by our perspective on the world. One third of Moskowitz's participants weren't aware that they preferred chunky sauce because they weren't aware that was what they liked.

If we go deeper than tomato sauce, Freud explained why sometimes, beyond the cognitive limitations of knowing ourselves, what we desire the most is sometimes the most difficult thing to divine about ourselves.

In simple terms, according to Freud, our ignorance of ourselves is created by the rejection of an experience. Before I explain this principle further, first it has to be understood that we consider an experience not only an objective fact, but anything we experience, like a desire, a feeling or a thought.

It is possible to consider all of those phenomena as an experience since they all have to be represented first in our psychic apparatus in order for us to be able to experience them at all. It is through this notion of representation that the idea of perspective or subjective position comes into play. Although it sounds complicated, what I'm trying to say is that what we experience in our lives is always observed from a particular point of view —what I have been referring to in this book as our subjective position— and that is this representation what we are able to perceive.

Real Object
—————————
Representation
—————————
Psychic Apparatus

That means that when we observe anything, like this book, what we see is a representation, formed thanks to our psychic apparatus. It is this same representation we can evoke when we can remember the book, without having it in front of us. The same thing happens with what we think or what we desire. After all, it's not necessary to have a delicious plate of pasta in front of us to desire to eat one. Most times it's enough to use our psychic apparatus and mental representations to imagine it, for the hunger to appear.

Some of these experiences are faced with a rejection by the individual, however, and that is the cause of the vast majority of the psychological problems that trouble us. But why does this rejection happen?

Freud tells us in *The Psychotherapy of Hysteria* that what these experiences have in common is that "they were altogether of that kind which one would not like to experience and prefers to forget."[4] The reason why is because "they were altogether of a painful nature adapted to provoke the affects of shame, reproach, of psychic pain, and the feeling of injury."[5]

But why do certain experiences produce those feelings of rejection? Because the representation of the experience was not compatible with those already organized in our ego, namely, it was not compatible with the idea that we have about ourselves. In the same book by Freud he explains that "an idea entered into the ego of the patient which proved to be unbearable and evoked a power of repulsion on the part of the ego, the purpose of which was a defense against this unbearable idea."[6]

I quote mostly *The Psychotherapy of Hysteria*, published in 1895, because it synthesizes the core idea of Freud's theory, the essence of which was maintained throughout his work.

At this point I would like to take an opportunity to clarify the mistaken idea that within psychoanalysis the only thing that really matters is our sexuality. As you can see, what is needed for something to be rejected by a person is the painful nature of the experience, such as horror, anxiety and shame. Although those feelings can be provoked by a situation of a sexual nature, all of us can easily imagine other kinds of situations that awaken terror in us, like the death of a loved one or a robbery, and also other thoughts or feelings, besides sexual ones, that could be incompatible with the values we hold as our own.

I have explained briefly why it is hard to know our own subjective position. First, there are the inherent limits of that position that make it difficult to see it in its entirety, insofar we all have cognitive biases and blind spots. And then secondly, and more pertinent to this discussion of psychotherapy, there are things about ourselves that we reject and prefer to forget, to not see, or not even to assume as our own.

Throughout his work Freud explained that most psychological symptoms are caused by a need to defend ourselves from representations that are unbearable in respect to the ones already gathered in our ego. Those representations incongruous with my beliefs regarding who I am are repelled and kept out of my conscience, and it is the process by which we manage this what causes distress and mental disorders.

An example of this is a woman that is not aware of her own flirtatious behavior, since she has always considered herself a loyal wife, or a man that demonstrates concern for a colleague and friend by telling her to relax and not work herself into the grave, without being able to acknowledge that he is also worried about her possible promotion and its impact on his own career. In the first case, we may find the woman and her husband asking for couples therapy because she is tired of her jealous partner. In the second, the man may visit us because he can't sleep but is unable to find the source of his worries.

For Freud, the unbearable nature of the representation has to do with "an ideal in himself by which he measures his actual ego, [an ideal that] arose from the critical influence of his parents (conveyed to him by the medium of the voice), to whom were added, as time went on, those who trained and taught him and the innumerable and indefinable host of all the other people in his environment —his fellow-men—and public opinion."[7]

This is a commonly accepted phenomenon. Our ideals come from our environment —at least in their beginning— and they greatly determine who we try to be, even if that means not assuming parts of true ourselves, especially those that go against such ideal.

Fortunately, Freud discovered that "through urging alone it would really be possible to bring to light the definitely existing pathogenic series of ideas."[8] That means that through his method —which I will explain briefly in the following pages— what was rejected by the patient can be brought to light. He often faced a resistance from his patients in his attempts accomplish this goal, however, and it is this resistance that makes up a central component of the cases I will talk about in this book. Freud made the following hypothesis: "through my psychic work I had to overcome a psychic force in the patient which opposed the pathogenic idea from becoming conscious (remembered). It then became clear to me that this must really be the same psychic force which assisted in the origin of the hysterical symptom, and at that time prevented the pathogenic idea from becoming conscious."[9]

In lay terms, when in the therapeutic work an attempt is made to bring the rejected representations to light, a resistance to the work can appear in different ways such as the commonly used drastic change of subject, an unproductive silence, or even harshly questioning the therapist or their qualifications.

It's not a surprise to face resistance if we try to make the rejected representation appear in a session, since we know it produced repulsion originally. This is why the key in all the cases —something that you will see in the following chapters of this book— is for the psychotherapist to know how to maneuver in such a way to avoid the awakening of this kind of resistance.

In summary, this rejection of an experience by patients — the rejection of a specific representation of a fact, of a thought, of a desire— was in fact "really a —more or less conscious— not willing to know, and the task of the therapist was to overpower this resistance of association by psychic labor."[10]

But how to do this work? We know that we can't get directly to the point, since it was previously rejected and direct intervention to undo the rejection will cause resistance from the patient. And, indeed, in some cases we may not even know what it was that was rejected, we may simply be aware of a rejection because of the symptoms it has caused. When Freud was starting to develop his method and was seeking to access rejected experiences in his patients, he first asked the patient to say what he thought of a particular issue, asking him to promise to communicate "this thought, no matter what it may be. He is not supposed to hold it back because he may perhaps think that it is not the desired or the right thing, or because it is too disagreeable to say. There should be neither criticism nor reserve on account of affect or disregard. Only thus could we find the things desired, and only thus have we unfailingly found them."[11]

In the early years of psychoanalysis, Freud ceased to ask this of his patients and started working with free association, a similar mechanism but in which the patient is not asked to associate about a particular issue, but just to say whatever comes to their mind.

With this procedure Freud attempted to "dissociate the attention of the patient from his conscious quest and reflection, in brief, from everything upon which his will can manifest itself."[12] It is a technique "serving to surprise for a while the defensive ego."[13]

It is key to remember the difference between what is said and the place from where it is said, since that subjective position appears and it is disclosed in different ways. Even if the session seems to dwell on an irrelevant topic —even unrelated to the patient's history, like a movie they saw on the weekend— it could be really all about their position, without them even noticing it.

The invitation to say whatever comes to mind encourages a freer speech, in which contents previously rejected can appear, in the safe space that the therapy creates.

In the same spirit we can find the interpretation of dreams —also commonly misunderstood— in which we take advantage of the fact that "on falling asleep the undesired ideas emerge, owing to the slackening of a certain arbitrary (and, of course, also critical) action, which is allowed to influence the trend of our ideas."[14]

We try to recover from the patient a rejected representation that appears in the dream wearing a disguise. A good example of this is when in the dream the patient is not them him- or herself but someone else —sometimes even a person they don't know— but that wishes and accomplishes exactly what the patient does not dare to recognize as theirs.

In this process dreams are used as nothing but an entrance —albeit a very important one for Freud— to utilize in our search for what has been rejected by the patient.

I previously mentioned that the way we listen as psychoanalysts is different than the regular way one listens to a friend or colleague. The reason behind this is that to really listen to the free association of the patient, something equivalent is required from their analyst. Since we don't know beforehand which topics will be the relevant ones, nor how a story connects with another, it is required from us to listen in a certain way. In Freud's words, this way of listening "consists simply in not directing one's notice to anything in particular and in maintaining the same 'evenly-suspended attention' (...) For as soon as anyone deliberately concentrates his attention to a certain degree, he begins to select from the material before him; one point will be fixed in his mind with particular clearness and some other will be correspondingly disregarded, and in making this selection he will be following his expectations or inclinations. This, however, is precisely what must not be done. In making the selection, if he follows his expectations he is in danger of never finding anything but what he already knows; and if he follows his inclinations he will certainly falsify what he may perceive. It must not be forgotten that the things one hears are for the most part things whose meaning is only recognized later on."[15]

This listening forces us to leave aside any kind of notes taken in the session, a practice so common in the psychologist offices nowadays, since they not only make the free association harder —if the therapist writes some of the things one says and not others, it's impossible to not have our free association affected— but it also makes it impossible to have an evenly-suspended attention, since we would be remembering and highlighting certain parts of the patient discourse, according to personal criteria that don't come from the subjective position of the person in front of us but from our own subjective interpretation and representation of what we are hearing.

This means that the way a psychotherapist should listen is simply to consider everything the patient says with the same merit, respecting their discourse without imposing prejudices or hypotheses about what is important, something that most of the time we will only know after listening to them. This type of therapy is, after all, an invitation to truly listen.

Finally, I would like to mention another key aspect of producing a change in our patients, an approach utilized in Freudian work since its inception. Although the rejection of a representation unbearable for the patient is the core of our patient's pain, Freud recognize that there is also "a secondary gain which appears in connection with other intentions of the ego, when the symptom is about to assert itself. It has also long been known to analysis that the withdrawal of this morbid gain, or the cessation of the same in consequence of some real change, is one of the mechanisms in the cure of the symptom."[16]

What does Freud mean with this secondary gain? Many times, even when it's not obvious, there is some unconscious benefit to our suffering. A good example is the larger amount of care a person could get when they are depressed. In Emily's case, she was visited much more frequently by her daughters now that she is sad because of her husband's passing, and maybe an unconscious reason to remain depressed are these visits. The same happens with the medical leaves, that may become an unconscious motivation to remain feeling ill. Like Freud said in the previous quote, sometimes it's enough to remove this secondary gain — eliminating the benefit— for the symptoms to disappear.

Another way to eliminate symptoms was cleverly exploited by the American psychiatrist and psychologist Milton Erickson, who in hundreds of ways was able to make the suffering of his patients to be much more costly for him to sustain than to finish it once and for all. One time he was treating a man with insomnia, and he told him that each night, before going to bed, he would have to wax the floors of his whole house. The first couple of nights the man did it and went to bed very late, as it was a big house and it took a long time to wax all the floors. However, before a week passed, he was falling asleep before waxing the floors and staying in bed until the next morning. Thus, you can see that despite the widely accepted idea that some kind of self-knowledge needs to happen in a psychotherapy, sometimes it's enough to modify the situation so the unconscious gain of the symptom disappears.

In the following chapters I will share with you ten cases to demonstrate some of the typical processes of psychotherapy mentioned in this chapter, like finding the subjective position of the patient, the place and manner of the interventions, and how they avoid the awakening of resistance, among other topics.

It's important to tell you that all of these cases were real patients I have treated, but I have modified the names, jobs, and other identifying information to maintain the confidentiality of the psychotherapeutic process. Additionally, the patients whose cases I have included have all been given the opportunity to read the chapter discussing their case and have authorized its publication. Since this book was originally written in Spanish, all quotes have also been translated into English.

In some of the cases the interventions eliminate the symptoms but don't act upon the cause of the problem, the rejected representation previously mentioned. In the therapeutic process, however, that is something I can work on with the patient in later sessions —and it was indeed addressed in most of the cases I discuss in this book once the symptoms causing problems in their daily life had been eliminated.

This means that a psychoanalysis, in its search for finding the subjective position of the patient so they can assume it and even modify it, results in different experiences that can have a range of therapeutic impacts, such as a sense of relief or the disappearance of a symptom, in a quick manner.

In short, what I will try to show in the following cases is that, in contrast to what many believe, people do change.

1. Lacan, Jacques. The seminar of Jacques Lacan. Book II: The Ego in Freud's theory and in the Technique of Psychoanalysis. Cambridge University Press, 1988.

2. Lacan, Jacques. The Seminar of Jacques Lacan: Book 1: Freud's Papers on Technique. Cambridge University Press, 1988.

3. Ibid.

4. Freud, Sigmund. Selected Papers on Hysteria and Other Psychoneuroses; Trans. by A. A. Brill. New York: The Journal of Nervous and Mental Disease Publishing Company, 1912.

5. Ibid.

6. Ibid.

7. Freud, Sigmund. On Narcissism: An Introduction. White Press, 2014.

8. Freud, Sigmund. Selected Papers on Hysteria and Other Psychoneuroses; Trans. by A. A. Brill. New York: The Journal of Nervous and Mental Disease Publishing Company, 1912.

9. Ibid.

10. Ibid.

11. Ibid.

12. Ibid.

13. Freud, Sigmund. The Interpretation of Dreams. Basic Books, 2010.

14. Ibid.

15. Freud, Sigmund. Complete Psychological Works Of Sigmund Freud, Vol 12. Vintage Classics, 2001.

16. Freud, Sigmund. The Collected Works of Sigmund Freud: Psychoanalytic Studies, Theoretical Essays & Articles. e-artnow, 2016.

II. MAKE ROOM FOR DEATH

One of the hardest moments in our lives is when we lose a person close to us. We often develop feelings of injustice about the world or are unable to find any sense in their passing, which fills us with anger. When the death was caused by an accident, it's possible that guilt appears, because of the remorse about things that could have been done differently to avoid such fate.

How does one deal with something like this? In this chapter I will share with you the experiences of a grieving woman who, with few interventions and a lot of patience and respect, was able to continue her life after the loss of her husband.

Patricia asked for an appointment over the phone, explaining to me that she was having trouble sleeping and that a friend had suggested to her that psychotherapy could help. When she arrived for the first session, she told me smiling that she had never slept well and had been taking sleeping pills prescribed by a neurologist for years. The pills had always worked well for her, but for three months she has slept poorly, even with the double dosage that her doctor had recommended.

When I asked her if she had any idea about what could have provoked this change, she told me *"nothing special happened three months ago"*, so she was surprised that the pills were no longer working.

To allow her subjective position appear, I began by starting to explore her history, asking about her family. She started to cry right away, telling me that her husband died six months ago of a heart attack and that she was still not recovered from that. While she was telling me all of that, she apologized profusely for her crying and told me she knew that *"by now this shouldn't be affecting me this much. After six months... this is not normal, right?"*

Even if it seems obvious, it's worth remembering that it is not the place of the psychotherapist to say what is normal and what is not, nor to explain to the patient the grieving process from the perspective of a specific theory. Our work is to understand the patient in their singularity, within their own story, allowing their subjective position to appear. Because of this goal, I simply showed myself to be perplexed about how she reached that idea, and invited her in this way to keep unfolding her story. Patricia told me then that her sisters, psychologist themselves, had explained to her that it wasn't normal for mourning to last that long.

It was clear to me that it was a good idea to leave unsolved the issue of whether it was normal or not to be affected by a loss six months later. After all, without even trying, I had already differentiated myself from the sisters who were adamant about her process being abnormal.

When Patricia started telling me about her sisters and their lives, I gently interrupted her and I asked her to tell me first about what happened to her husband. In this way, without explicitly stating it, I was showing her that it was something that we should talk about, whether it was normal or not.

John was her husband for almost thirty years. Patricia told me that his great pleasure was the food she made. *"Everyone always tells me 'you are a great cook' "*, she explained, and started enumerating all the desserts she made almost daily.

On a Saturday like any other, after the two of them had dinner, John felt a sharp pain in his chest, and despite Patricia immediately calling an ambulance, the doctors at the hospital were not able to save his life.

There was so much paperwork to do, between banks, hospital bills and the funeral services, that for the first month she couldn't sit down to cry. Her three daughters, all independent adults, asked her to handle everything because they were *"too sad to function."*

In the following two months Patricia was able to cry. Every night at least one of her daughters joined her for dinner and they talked about John. After that time, however, her daughters grew tired of her suffering, telling her to stop crying, and that if the only topic of conversation would be their late father they would stop going for dinner. *"Again?"* her daughters told her when she forgot and talked about her husband.

Nevertheless, Patricia was still very upset, mainly because she felt responsible. *"The heart attack was because of his cholesterol... maybe if I wouldn't have indulged him in everything, doing those desserts every day... maybe he would still be alive."* She told me that in a checkup with his cardiologist, the doctor had recommended a change in his diet, but that she *"couldn't say no to his pouting."*

Without a doubt, the most shocking statement she said in her first session, and that she would repeat in following encounters, was: *"In a way, I killed him."*

Here we can see a statement that clearly reflected her subjective position towards what happened, that key that I mentioned in the first chapter, that will allow us to understand a patient and be able to work with them.

If we take this specific position into account, it's not strange at all that Patricia was still suffering and having trouble sleeping. However, her sisters and daughters repeated to her again and again that *"a grieving process shouldn't take more than six months,"* and because of this, they were bothered if they saw Patricia was sad. For this reason, lately she had attempted to avoid crying around them, even hiding it when her daughters were at home. *"When I do the laundry I take the chance to cry... the noise of the machine hides it."*

When Patricia asked me if it was normal to keep crying, I told her that it seemed there was still a lot to cry about. She told me she felt sad, *"thinking where is he now... if I could have done something different... if I will see him again."*

We then further explored these thoughts, discussing how she imagined the place where her husband could be, if she could have in fact done something different to save his life, and other things that you have to speak about when someone dies like that, no matter how much time has passed since the death.

If there was something crucial to talk about it was her position, reflected as we saw in the statement, *"In a way, I killed him."* Many people, and more than a few psychotherapists, consider it negative to make room to speak about guilt in a case like this. They believe that will only make the guilt grow. However, the exact opposite is true.

To talk about her guilt, to have the space to examine her ideas about it, without anyone trying to calm her with clichés, is the only way to make that feeling go away. The key to this case, like in most grieving and traumatic processes, is to be patient and give the other person the time to talk, as many times as they need, about their pain. There can't be any rush, there can't be any deadline.

Death affects all of us so deeply we often try to make the pain go away swiftly, to keep its damage limited to a superficial level, thereby limiting the degree to which we are touched by that death, and avoiding having to face the reality that it will happen to us someday too. When listening to someone else's grief we often try to calm the other person, denying them the possibility to feel what they are feeling in that moment, to avoid having to recognize the presence of death in our everyday life.

"What do you feel guilty about? Don't be foolish," her daughters told her, trying to calm their mother. But Patricia told me that the lack of understanding from them was yet another reason for her suffering.

We spent a couple of sessions talking about John, of her memories of their life together, of the night of the heart attack, of the guilt she felt about her desserts. We spoke of all of this without any rush, giving her room to examine every idea no matter how illogical it may have sounded. She apologized often because she was still suffering, and each time I had to show her that she had every right to still be suffering.

Bit by bit, Patricia started to ask herself about her future. At first she was worried and sad about continuing life without her husband but nevertheless, she was willing to look ahead. This was a change from the discourse focused on her husband's death, to one speaking about what was to come and the things she dreamt of doing. Without proposing it directly, just by giving her time and space to vent without restriction, Patricia started speaking less frequently about John, was able to sleep more, and saw the relationship with her daughters improved.

The guilt was also disappearing, something that was clear when she told me she had begun to prepare desserts again, this time for her grandchildren. *"But I will make healthier versions of them,"* she said at the end of one session.

When we were finishing her treatment Patricia was planning a trip with her daughters, who *were "happy that mom is thinking positively."* She was no longer feeling guilty, because she was able to recognize for herself other factors that contributed to John's death: he didn't just eat her desserts every day but also had fast food every day at work, had never played any sports, and refused her invitations to join her at the gym. One of the last things she told me with a smile on her face was: *"How foolish I was to think that I killed him."*

It's not a surprise to learn that Patricia's sleeping problems disappeared as she worked through her grief, and that she was even able to lower the dosage of the pills she had taken for years, even lower than before John's death.

Although the goal of psychotherapy can be summed up as the questioning of the subjective position, we have to remember that one has to be respectful of the rhythm and acceptable pacing of the needs of patient. If we push them too fast or too hard, we run the risk of awakening resistance in the individual which can result in the vigorous defense of their current position. I highlight this because in certain traumatic cases, unlike with Patricia, the patient may not seem affected at all, because of the shock they can be numb and thus apparently unaffected by the death of a loved one.

In those cases it's not indicated to intervene by trying to convince the patient that they should be affected. Even if it's possible that venting and speaking about the traumatic event would help them, it is crucial to wait for the right time for that. Common mistakes are saying things like: *"You must be suffering, but it's hard for you to recognize it"*, *"You have an armor that doesn't let you feel,"* or even *"Are you sure you are not affected by what happened?"*

What do we do then? When the patient is numb or not allowing themselves to feel, we don't have to push them to feel more, but can instead explore the fact that they don't feel; our questions can be about the fact that they are not feeling, about the reasons of that apparent dissociation. Sometimes, a simple: *"Why do you think you don't feel affected?"* provokes as an answer an opening in their position, a connection with the emotion caused by the trauma. More than once, confronted by a question as simple as that, a patient has answered me with *"because it would be too painful."*

It is a subtle difference, but notice that I did not ask, *"Why do you think you were not affected?"*, which allows the possibility of them not being affected. I asked *"Why do you think you don't feel affected?"*, that already tells them they are, but they don't feel it.

Time and again these kinds of interventions show us that, without needing sophisticated techniques, the patient lowers their defenses and achieves the connection with what they are feeling and thinking, and thus we can begin working on that. Speaking about why it would be too painful to feel affected can thus allow us to build bridges to the trauma itself.

In summary, in psychotherapy a key element is being patient with the rhythm of the other person, something that is even more important in cases that revolve around trauma. By following their lead we avoid re-traumatizing our patient by abstaining from forcing them to talk about what they prefer to forget, or forcing them to explore a painful experience at a rate or depth that produces more pain for them. Respecting their pace, we allow the subjective position to appear and we are able to intervene to produce a shift in it, thus producing a change in the patient's symptoms and beyond.

We, therefore, have to make room for the patient's pain, for the trauma, and even for the uncomfortable topic of death in our discussions.

III. THE BETRAYAL OF CATS

One of the conditions that often brings people to psychotherapy is the experience of a phobia. A simple definition of a phobia is: an intense and irrational fear triggered by the presence of an object or situation which provokes anxiety and complicates the daily life of a person. Typical examples of those fears include being afraid of: flying on an airplane, specific animals (i.e. snakes or spiders), or being in enclosed spaces. It is important to remember that the phobic fear can even be triggered by the anticipation of an object or situation, that is, without even confronting it directly. This is the case we will examine below, in which although the afflicted person acknowledges that her fear is irrational and excessive, she still cannot avoid it.

A couple of years ago I treated Jennifer, a forty-nine years old woman, seeking help with a specific phobia. When we started working together, the first thing she told me was: *"I want to get rid of my fear of cats."*

Jennifer stated that she knew her fear was *"way too stupid"* but she had still been living with this phobia for almost ten years. She said she decided to address this problem now because it had gotten worse: at first she did not like touching cats, thinking she might get bitten by them, but by the time she came to me she was afraid of walking on the streets of her hometown, for fear of running into a cat.

Throughout the session, she commented several times about how *"stupid"* this situation seemed to her and, later on, admitted that one of the reasons why she had not gone to a psychotherapist before was that she was ashamed to tell a stranger about her fear.

In the first session she explained that this phobia *"started out of the blue"* as she had never had a negative experience with cats, *"I have known people who begin to be afraid of dogs after they got bitten. That is understandable but it's not my case."*

Her family didn't know what to do, since her fear of cats had increased to the point of her not being able to work. Jennifer said to me: *"I avoid the streets where I could run into one of them. The problem is that there are so many, that I am not able to move around the city."*

What should we, as therapists, do in this case? We must listen to Jennifer's words and try to find the position from where she speaks. By listening in this way we can help her move from that subjective position to find one in which she no longer needs this symptom.

Using a purposefully innocent tone, at the end of the first session I asked her what she associated with cats.

With a serious look, Jennifer replied, *"they are treacherous."*

This statement became one of three phrases that directed my work with Jennifer: *"get rid of my fear"*, *"too stupid"*, and *"they are treacherous."* I will explain the significance of these three declarations as we move further through this case study.

At our second session I started to ask Jennifer about her life, including her family and work, before she developed this phobia. Even though I told her the reason I was asking was to understand her background, in truth I was also looking for other factors that could be associated with her phobia.

To summarize what she told me, the patient had been married to her husband, Joe, for thirty years, she had three daughters in their twenties, and she did not see any problems in her life other than her phobia. She stated that she did not miss her job as a secretary since, *"at this point the money that my husband makes is enough for us."* In short, at first sight, everything seemed to be going well in her life.

At the end of this session she asked me when we would start the treatment to cure her phobia. What Jennifer did not know was that her treatment had already started.

My insistence that she told me her story was beneficial, and by the third session, the issue of treachery came up again, but not in reference to her feared cats. In discussing her life Jennifer stated, *"I haven't had betrayals in my life, though many people wouldn't agree with me."*

When I asked her what she meant by that, she explained that her friends have told her several times that her husband was cheating on her. Even their daughters believed it so. Nevertheless, every time she confronted Joe, he had some excuse and made Jennifer believe in him again.

"Although everyone tells me that Joe is cheating on me, I do not believe it... my friends are now even telling me that I am stupid." Here we can see the word *"stupid"* again, the same word she used many times to define her phobia, this time used in reference to her trust in her husband.

Jennifer chose to follow this thread in the next few sessions and continued talking about her husband, rather than her phobia. In one session, she said that if there was something with which she had to agree with others in her life, it was that her husband *"tricked"* her.

When I asked her about this, she explained that Joe is a lawyer and when Jennifer's mother died some years ago, he took care of her mother's inheritance: *"My sisters were the ones who first told me something... Joe charged too much for the procedures and paperwork that he was supposed to do. In the end we have spent so much money that they asked another lawyer. He told them that Joe defrauded us, that the fee should not have been as high as Joe told us."*

I invited her to continue, surprised by the fact there wasn't just one but now two—at the very least— possible betrayals from her husband.

"When we confronted him, Joe accused me of being disloyal, that I did not trust him and he said he would no longer work on the case. He never returned a dime, because according to him, he had spent it on paperwork and the time he had spent on the matter. I felt betrayed."

In contrast to her statements about Joe's purported infidelity, in this instance Jennifer considers his 'treacherous' behavior a fact. I asked her when all of this had happened and she replied that it occurred ten years before. I then asked when the possible infidelity had occurred. *"That same year,"* she replied.

In the next sessions she told me other parts of the story with her husband without any mention of her phobia. Sometimes she mentioned again how stupid it was to have been defrauded. Stupid for not realizing that he might be unfaithful. Stupid for having forgiven him. And, above all, stupid for having tolerated him all this time.

I stopped her at this point simply saying: *"Why did you?"* The answer to this question clarified what was happening:

"It was fear. Ten years ago my daughters were not independent like they are now. Joe was the support of our house. I had to look the other way, and try to forget what he had done. I had to put distance between me and my sisters, who couldn't stand my husband anymore. My friends kept telling me I shouldn't be stupid, that I needed to face him on the subject of lovers. But in the end I decided to ignore it."

Jennifer's words show in a clear way the mechanism of phobia. Faced with a reality we do not want to deal with, we decide not to assume a position which would force us to do it. Instead, we move the feeling of the problem to another issue, usually connected to the true source of the fear by some hidden logic.

Ignoring the problem by developing the phobia, Jennifer unconsciously decided to worry about the treacherous cats instead of her treacherous husband.

After discussing her husband's behavior and her choice not to confront him over the course of the four sessions, she mentioned she was no longer afraid of cats, that she had seen some on the street and didn't experience any feeling of anxiety. Despite this 'cure' for her initial reason for seeking therapy, however, she kept coming to her appointments, trying to find the courage to confront her fear of facing her husband's behavior.

It took her a couple of months but she did it. After a long conversation at home between the two of them, her husband admitted that he, in fact, had been having an affair for years. He even confessed that he used part of the fraudulent fee from her inheritance legal work to continue maintaining this double life.

In the sessions following this conversation Jennifer cried a lot. You might think she cried a great deal over Joe's betrayal of their marriage but most of her tears were shed over the fact that it took her so long to face her fear. Little by little, as we continued our work after her talk with Joe, Jennifer told her story once again and this time she was able to see, for herself, the evidence of all that had happened. At the same time, she began to talk about her future and what might lie in store in light of finally confronting Joe's infidelity and 'treacherous' behavior.

At the end of the treatment, Jennifer was not living with her husband anymore; she was happily living alone with a cat.

IV. THE FREEDOM OF NOT EATING

Eating disorders are becoming increasingly more common in our society. In many cases, however, the often severe behavior of anorexia or bulimia hides other underlying issues and the only way to treat the individual effectively is to address both the eating disorder and the deeper issues at the same time. In this chapter I will show how a change in the subjective position of the patient, through the change in her family dynamic, was used in this type of treatment.

A couple of years ago I got an email from a worried mother in which she told me that her fifteen year-old daughter, Elizabeth, was suffering from anorexia. The teenager had been treated for an eating disorder in the past, and supposedly cured by the interventions of a nutritionist and a psychiatrist. However, two years later, this mother was watching her daughter return to her old habits which had resulted in a rapid decline in Elizabeth's weight. She finished her email by asking me for an appointment for Elizabeth and adding that besides the anorexia, she thought that her daughter was much more complicated than other girls her age.

To understand the situation as well as I could, and to assess the worry of the mother, I invited only her to the first session. In most cases, it is a good idea to meet first with the person that is asking for the appointment, whether or not they are actually the potential patient.

Why would I do this, you might ask? Since they are the one who thinks psychotherapy is needed, we will be able to learn what makes them think that, and to assess if it would be a good idea to include them in the treatment along with the person they are worried about.

In that first session the mother told me that two years ago Elizabeth was well below her usual weight and that it was only after having her hospitalized and in outpatient treatment for a year that she was able to return to a healthy weight. A couple of months prior to her contacting me the mother started to notice that Elizabeth was eating less and less, and had begun steadily losing weight. She even told me that during one of her regular checks of Elizabeth's room she read her daughter's diary and found that her diet contained only lettuce with some lemon juice. That information was the last straw that made her seek my help.

Here is another reason why it can be useful to have the first session with the individual requesting the therapy, without the potential patient: sometimes there is relevant information they will only share if they are alone with the psychotherapist. In this case, it was knowledge gleaned from the reading of her daughter's diary that she might not have disclosed with her daughter present, but that revelation allowed me to understand why she asked for an appointment at that particular time.

She commented that, in addition to struggling with the eating disorder, she had her daughter *"under control"* because she was also diagnosed with attention-deficit disorder. In dealing with this other issue, Elizabeth had been in neurological treatment for years, and her mother forced her to study a couple of hours every day. Throughout this session it eventually became clear to me that one of the topics to explore in this case would be the control that the mother exerted over her daughter.

I asked Elizabeth to come alone for the second session, to get to know her perspective on the situation. The teenager recognized that she had an eating disorder a couple of years ago, but she thought that at the time of the session there was not a problem except for the overreaction of her mother. When we met, Elizabeth was eight pounds under her usual weight. She told me then that her mother insisted that she eat all day and that she brought food to Elizabeth's room even when she had said she was not hungry.

Her mother didn't like the meals they gave Elizabeth at the school cafeteria, since they were not healthy enough in her opinion, so every day she gave her daughter a home-made lunch to take. The first thing that her mother asked when she picked Elizabeth up from school was, *"did you eat your lunch?"* This repeated questioning was something that Elizabeth said she was *"fed up"* about. *"I am tired that food is such an issue… one day, just one day, she could just not ask me about it."*

The issue of control, that I observed in the first session with the mother, clearly appeared in the discourse of her daughter. She said she was tired of being treated *"like a baby."* Other examples of control that Elizabeth mentioned in her session included her mother not letting her go out most of the time and her need to determine with which friends Elizabeth could get together.

I had in front of me a teenager with a possible eating disorder but, at the same time, my patient was a teenager under strict control by the mother, yearning for freedom. That was where I found the lever to provoke a change.

Taking into account that she was tired of food being an issue —an issue for which she already had completed treatment— I proposed this to Elizabeth: *"since you don't have a problem with food, and you're tired of your mother making it an issue, I will ask her to come alone next week, and tell her that for a month she can't mention the subject."* Incredulous, she asked me how I would accomplish that.

I explained that her mother would need some kind of proof to believe that under this arrangement things were not going to get worse. I asked her for her help: *"how about if I tell your mom to not say anything about food for a month, while I treat you, but we all agree that if you lose weight or even just maintain your current weight it means that the treatment isn't working? Can you try to help me with this and work on gaining 100 grams a week?"*

Elizabeth did the math herself, and told me she didn't have a problem with my plan, since that meant that in a month she wouldn't gain even one pound. She thought it was a fair price to pay to be free of her mother's control over her food.

I suggested this intervention as I thought that her position regarding food was caused by a rebellion, because of the fatigue about it being an issue, more than about losing weight. If I was right, just by removing the cause to rebel, a change should happen naturally. But why 100 grams specifically? First of all, it's such a small amount that I assumed Elizabeth would not say no to the idea. My second reason was that while it is a small amount, if a person tries to gain a hundred grams it is probable that they will gain a bit more. Between these two factors, therefore, I believed that Elizabeth would be able to return to a healthy weight at a pace that wouldn't frighten her.

In the third session I proposed this deal to the mother, who accepted it without much hope. For the mother, the issue that needed to be resolved was Elizabeth eating enough food, not her right to assert control over her own life or any other topic that might be impacting her desire to eat.

In the fourth session the three of us met together for the first time, two weeks after Elizabeth's agreement to my deal. Instead of the 200 grams she was to have gained, she had increased her weight by 500 grams. This was not a problem for her, however, she told me with a smile that *"it doesn't matter, it's only 300 grams more."* She was eating better and was less worried about the subject. Above all, she was very grateful that her mother stopped questioning her about it.

Elizabeth's mother did not talk much in that session. She confessed that it had been hard to not ask about her daughter's nutrition, and that gaining one pound in two weeks was not something that we should celebrate, since Elizabeth was still under her normal weight. I invited her to honor our deal as long as Elizabeth kept increasing by 100 grams a week, since we at least agreed we were moving in the right direction. Before leaving, Elizabeth told me that she was selected to play on the field hockey team at her high school, something that her mother approved of with a smile, saying, *"it's something to be proud of."*

The following week, Elizabeth not only maintained her new weight, but increased it again by approximately 200 grams. The mother was also keeping her end of the deal, and was recognizing the changes in her daughter.

However, as it often happens in human relationships, if one of the elements begins to change, the other changes too. In this session Elizabeth's mother told us that she wanted her daughter to return home from school by herself. She was tired of picking her up every day, especially since she was finishing school at a different time than her brothers because of hockey practice. Elizabeth did not want to return home by bus because it would take longer to get home, leaving her with less time to study.

I finished the session with the following suggestion: *"I propose that now that we know that you can handle your nutrition like an adult, this month we keep asking your mother to not tell you anything food related, but in exchange you return home by bus."* They both agreed to this plan and the mother repeated the agreement before leaving, making it clear that the weight gain was still on the table as well: *"I won't bother you with food, if you keep gaining weight and return by bus from school, so we'll all be happy."*

It is subtle, but if you look at my suggestion, you will find the statement *"we know that you can handle your nutrition,"* as part of the agreement, something that the mother did not deny this time. The message to the decentred level mentioned in the first chapter, the level in which we work in therapy, was thus reached, and the change in the subjective position highlighted to both of them.

The subjective position of the mother in relation to her daughter's eating, and others topics, was of one of maintaining control. The kind of control we would expect from the mother of a small child, not of a teenager. Confronted with this, the daughter rebelled in the same plane, not eating just to resist the mother's inappropriate control, something we see frequently in small children.

Once it is undeniable that the daughter can handle her nutrition, and that considering her a grownup would free the mother of other responsibilities (like having to pick her up at school instead of taking the bus), the subjective position of both individuals shifts. The mother finally sees her daughter as the fifteen year-old that she is, and at the same time the daughter can behave like one.

A month later I saw them both again at my office.

Elizabeth was up two pounds, eating healthy food, and still happy with her new life. And at only four pounds underweight, instead of the eight she was at the beginning of the treatment, her mother was proud of her daughter, and happy to see the chance of an eating disorder relapse fading away.

V. MAKE THE TIME: HOW DO YOU DEAL WITH AN EXHAUSTING WORKLOAD?

What do we understand about stress? Although it generally has a negative connotation, stress is an adaptive organism's reaction to a situation that is perceived as either a threat or too demanding, functioning positively to motivate the organism to seek a change in that situation. Even though it is a natural reaction, when the duration of the stressful situation extends over time, the body can become overcharged with tension, which can cause discomfort and even certain diseases.

Let's take the case of Richard, who arrived at my office telling me that because he had worked for years at a very demanding job, he felt stressed all year long. What worried him the most is that he felt tired all day, but at night it was hard to fall asleep. He told me that he didn't like his job, not because of what he had to do there —mostly calculations that he found truly interesting— but because of how exhausted it made him feel.

When I asked him about his daily routine, he explained that he left his house every day around 7 am, and that he returned from work around 8 pm. Because of his job responsibilities, however, most days he had to continue working once he got home, eating something while sitting at the computer. When he was finally able to go to bed, it was hard for him to relax and he couldn't help thinking about what he had to do the next day. Many times he was not able to fall asleep until well after midnight.

In part because of this stressful life, Richard had been divorced a couple of years before and he now lived alone in an apartment near work. His wife had left him telling him that she wasn't *"interested in a workaholic."* He had visitation rights to see his son every weekend, but usually he did not have time for a visit.

When I asked him if, besides work, he did anything else during the day, specifically something he liked, he replied: *"I don't have time for anything."* He repeated this answer when I asked about the weekend or even about his holidays.

In my opinion, the key to this case was his constant complaint about not having time for anything. This statement is an excessive generalization, since it's always possible to have some time to do something besides work, even if that something is just listening to one song you like. If you think about it, you can always wake up five minutes earlier to have that time, or take a short five minute break when you get home from work. Richard, however, was sure it was impossible. He constantly repeated that he didn't have time left to pursue activities he enjoyed nor to unwind. He only had time to work, do the house chores, and sleep.

I asked him if it was possible to have just 15 minutes a day for himself. He recalled again all the things he did every day, things that for him made it impossible to have even those 15 minutes. Taking advantage of his love for mathematics, which he disclosed when discussing his job, I asked him what percentage of the day was made up of 15 minutes. *"Around one percent,"* he said with a smile.

Let's stop here for a second to highlight how an intervention has to adjust to the patient's singularity; the same intervention doesn't work for every patient because everyone's subjective position is different. If Richard had not been skilled in math, the same question would not have been as effective, and it could have even complicated the session since it could have been hard for him to make that calculation. Additionally, because it was something that appealed to his personal abilities and interests, it had the added benefit of 'speaking his language' and appealing to him on a personal level. In this way I was able to tailor the intervention to his particular experience.

Let's continue with the case to find out how this individualized intervention played out. When Richard realized that we were only talking about one percent of the day he changed his mind and became open to the possibility of taking those 15 minutes daily. We talked about the different things he would like to do during that time. It was hard for Richard to come up with something. *"It has been so long since I have done something I like, I don't even know what I like to do,"* he told me. Finally he said that he would like to cook a more elaborate meal for himself, browse websites not related to work, or watch 15 minutes of a TV series.

The next week he told me that in fifteen minutes he was unable to do anything. I asked him if taking the time off each day had affected his work, his chores, or his rest. Richard told me *"of course not. One percent is negligible"*, so obviously it wouldn't affect anything. Even though he reported not doing anything in those daily fifteen minutes, as we talked I came to realize that Richard had in fact done something: he had thought of many other things he did want to do.

As you can see, thinking of activities he would like to do, something that had been almost impossible the previous week, had then become a natural occurrence during this window of unassigned time. This demonstrates how taking some distance from our stressors can allow us to examine what we enjoy in life, an important first step to be able to relax and be happier.

Coming up with things he wanted to do did not solve Richard's problems, however, as his other previous complaints were still present. All the things he had thought of that he wanted to do, unsurprisingly, took more than fifteen minutes, a realization that left him feeling hopeless; he was not going to be able to do them because he was not willing to allocate more than one percent of his day to relaxation. He had started the treatment in a subjective position that we can find in his statement: *"I don't have time for anything."* After one session, it had been shifted to allow one percent of the day to do something besides work. It was time to another shift, this time in how the percentage was allocated.

Again I used his love for math to help me present my planned intervention. *"How much time would you need to do the things you want to do?"* I asked.

"Around one hour," he replied with a sad face.

Among the activities that he thought of, I chose the one that seemed the easiest for him, riding his bike, and I told him that the assignment for the week was doing that.

He pointed out, a bit angry, that he didn't have time for that, repeating all the things he had to do every day.

Ready for this argument, I then explained my plan to him, *"Right now you are taking 105 minutes off a week [15 minutes each of the seven days of the week], thus if you take 60 minutes to ride your bike, you will have 45 minutes still available in the week. Why don't you take 15 minutes to rest on Monday, Wednesday and Friday, and then on Saturday you ride your bike for an hour?"*

As you can see, the key to this case was going step by step, starting with asking him to make an almost negligible change in taking only 15 minutes a day that did not leave room for his usual perspective of *"there is no time"*. Converting this time into a percentage of the hours of a day reinforced this notion, since almost every one of us think that one percent of something is practically nothing. And then, once he had accepted that change, it was easier for him to agree to rearranging them in the way I proposed. After all, as he had told me many times in the first session, Richard was *"a man of numbers."*

What do you think happened the following week? Richard arrived telling me that he was happy because he had ridden his bike to a nearby mountain that weekend. He had enjoyed the ride but told me that he couldn't have done it if he followed our arrangement as his ride had taken more than an hour of his week.

Because of my desire to avoid triggering resistance in him, a goal that you may remember I discussed in the first chapter, I played the Devil's advocate hoping to help him come to his own conclusions about how to solve this problem. I therefore asked him many times, acting surprised, if he was really sure that one percent a day was not enough. He finally said that he had really thought about it and, though if he respected my professional opinion, he considered my one percent was too little. He felt strongly that it should be two percent.

I told him that he could try this week with that number, that is, three breaks of 30 minutes in the week, and 2 hours to ride his bike on the weekend.

The next session, Richard told me that he had decided that five percent of the week to do the things he liked was the ideal number, that is, 8 hours. He brought a proposal to me: 30 minutes each day of the work week, and five and a half hours on the weekend. In fact, he had already planned to go to a football game with his son, who Richard told me couldn't believe that he had *"made the time"*.

When I saw him the following week, for the first time since we had started our work together he didn't start the session telling me how stressed and tired he was. Instead, he told me in detail how the day with his son had been, and the plans he had for the following weeks. And as for his stress symptoms, he told me he was sleeping better, something that he attributed to the tiredness caused by riding his bike. Above all, he told me, he was happy to see more of his son, and he felt he had more energy during the day.

Two weeks after that, I wasn't surprised to see a man who appeared even less stressed. He truly had been able to shift his perception of his use of time to allow himself the necessary rejuvenating and relaxing activities that he had been lacking in his life. It may be a small change, but by changing how we talk about our time use and allowing ourselves to have one percent of the day instead of zero can change our lives. Often, as we have seen with Richard's case, when we don't see a way to change our situation, our subjective position is the issue we have to work on first, looking at how we see and understand the problem, not just the problem itself, is what leads to helpful change.

"I want to recover the time I lost," he said when the session was ending.

How can we explain what happened? I think that what Richard's son said is the best way: he made the time.

VI. A Loneliness that Entangles

A couple of years ago I treated Nick, a young man of twenty years old. I think his is an interesting case because it shows very clearly that the key in the early stages of treatment is not to diagnose a specific pathology —such as depression— but to allow the subjective positions to appear and to listen to the patient, to make room for their sorrows and their fears.

This difficulty in distinguishing between normal struggles in life and the beginning of something more serious appeared in the first thing Nick told me: *"Look, it's not easy to explain, it's nothing concrete, but it's sad... it's sad what's happening to me, it's kind of stupid and childish. I came because I feel alone... for a long time now. It's not that I don't have friends, though I don't have many, but it doesn't have to do with that. It doesn't matter if I am with a lot of people or not... I feel alone either way, like it's something coming from within."*

Hearing what he said as I established my first idea of what he was dealing with, I noted that what was happening to him was not new, that it had been happening *"for a long time."* When I asked him about his loneliness, however, he replied explaining it didn't feel the same way as before: *"I know that in fact we're all alone, in an existentialist sense I have always known that, but it feels different now... as if the loneliness has become sticky, gooey... it's harder to endure, but at the same time, it's becoming more and more comfortable not interacting with people."*

While he had felt some of this *"for a long time now"*, it also clearly appeared that there had been a change: his usual loneliness had turned into something else, something difficult to endure. I asked him to explain what he meant by sticky. Why? Because in contrast to the daily loneliness he referred to at the beginning of the session, which seemed like a personal preference from his existentialist comment, when he talked about loneliness becoming thick or gooey, his worry appeared.

"Yeah, sticky… like it catches me and I get stuck in that. When I feel alone, each time I feel more alone… I study marketing, where we have to do group assignments, and that is getting harder, it's hard to tolerate people… it's not that they bother me, it is that they bore me… I don't know if I am making myself clear."

The tension between two subjective positions appeared there once again. First, he talked about this new feeling related to loneliness as something that catches him, and then he downplayed it saying it was simply about boredom.

Without a doubt, this fluctuation between those two positions was partially explained because of his fear of what was going on with him. Many times at the early stages of depression the person feels something akin to what Nick was describing, that is, we feel something strange, as if the depression has a strength of its own that takes us, even overwhelms us. It is crucial that as psychotherapists we do not attempt to downplay what is going on with the patient, reinforcing for example in this case the position that there is nothing else but his natural tendency to be alone.

On the contrary, it was key to emphasize that he was talking about something different from what was happening to him before, that is, there was something going on beyond his natural tendency. The intervention I therefore chose was direct: *"It seems it's not just your natural tendency, but something else. When did you start feeling like this?"*

After we had explored this new sensation more extensively, I shifted subjects to get to know more about Nick's individual context. I wanted to find out what could have caused this worsening in his feeling of loneliness. When he spoke about his family some issues appeared that were going to be important for the following sessions:

"Before sitting at the table you have to know that you will hear a series of complaints and problems... we never talk about anything positive. I'm not an optimist, but if we're going to talk about problems, let's talk about the big ones, real ones. I'm not going to sit and tell my mom 'I feel alone', because I would feel like a crybaby, and there is nothing she can do about it, so I would only bother her."

There we found two possible approaches to the case, that is, to focus the session on his feelings of loneliness, or to explore in more detail his family situation. I chose the latter, mostly because I thought it would raise less resistance in a first session, but I was also attempting to discover what could have produced the change in Nick.

When I asked him more about his mother, he replied: *"She can't handle anything else because she always has problems. If she knew that I felt alone, she would get upset, because she is always telling me to do more things that people of my age do, that I should go out more, that I should meet some 'girls'. Maybe she realizes I am lonely, more alone than I would like, and she is pressuring me to be different.*

She always has people invited for tea and things like that, my sister is the same... I am the loner of the family."

There are at least two aspects to what he said that could be important for this case. First, the mother was always having problems. It would be interesting to know what kind of troubles Nick was talking about, to see if they were affecting him too. At the same time, he was putting himself in opposition to his family in the core subject of loneliness, stating that while his family is sociable, he is *"the loner."* Because it was the first session and the time was almost up, I preferred to start inquiring about the first topic, because I thought it would raise less resistance in him. Besides that, if there was a serious family issue, it would also be important to know that as soon as possible.

It was, however, quickly made clear by Nick that the problems that troubled his mother were not connected to his loneliness, nor did they sound serious, at least according to his view. *"She even gets stressed about what to wear the next day,"* he told me.

Once the first session was over, it was clear to me that the core issue in this case was this new feeling of loneliness, and that it was going to be important in the following sessions to give him room to talk about that *"sticky"* loneliness, as well as opening for discussion the topic of the difference he felt between himself and his family.

In the second session I asked him about his statement of being *"the loner"* in opposition to the sociability of the rest of the members of his family. Nick got emotional and explained that his mother *"doesn't accept that I am just different... my parents work in marketing too, and they are always telling me about how they were the life of the party, that they always had people around them, doing stuff, that they find that healthy... so indirectly they are telling me I am sick."*

That appeared to be a key issue for Nick. He was not only different from his family, but he believed his natural tendency was seen as unhealthy by his parents. If we added to that his growing feeling of loneliness, we could understand his reluctance to accept that something was getting worse.

We kept talking about his family, particularly the differences between him and the other members. At the end of the session, he told me that his father had a similar opinion about him as his mother: *"My dad usually tells me 'you are not going to tell me that you prefer to watch a movie in your room than go out to a party, that is not normal.' I just keep my mouth shut because I don't have any interest in arguing with him, and at the end I do what I want either way. That's one of the things that bothers me about people, that they feel they have the right to question me. Why do they have to care about how I live my life? I feel ok being how I am... if I come here it's not to change that, but to avoid how the loneliness grabs me tight and I end up isolated from everyone... that is the only thing I am afraid of."*

After naming the fear, without giving me a chance to intervene, his subjective position oscillated again, *"I wouldn't like that because of a natural tendency of mine I ended up too far away from everyone... it's a battle against the comfortableness of my loneliness."* As you can see, in that session the two positions kept alternating, creating that tension I already noted between differing perceptions on what was happening: considering his attitude towards his loneliness as a natural tendency or accepting that what he was feeling was not normal, that it was something different than the usual loneliness.

The key to helping Nick was clearly going to be to help him differentiate between those two positions, both valid but referring to two different things. Nick could have a natural tendency to enjoy loneliness more than his family and friends but, even if he was afraid to confront it, he had to accept that what was going on now was something beyond that. This new feeling was something moving dangerously towards the early stage of depression and, more importantly, was something that scared him.

How to intervene in a case like this? It was important to empathize with the fear he felt towards the experience he was living, but still encourage him by giving him space and time to explore it.

In the third session I focused on that, giving him the chance to talk about the sticky loneliness he was feeling. During that session Nick told me that he knew that *"something is happening to me, and I don't know what will happen to me,"* and I could see this was a topic on which I would have to insist we maintain our focus.

His mother appeared again in his discourse, like in many sessions that would follow, mostly talking about how she keeps insisting that he needs to *"have a life"*. Nick also spoke about his dad saying that when he is *"sad or mad, I just lock myself up in my room and that's it. My dad knocks many times and asks what's going on, but I know he is not going to understand. The few times I tried to explain my fears to him, he had reprimanded me for being bothered for such small things... the common phrase that 'there are people that have it worse than you' and things like that."*

Because every time his natural tendency to loneliness appeared this trait was rejected and misunderstood by his family, it was not surprising that he preferred not to share his new worry with his family, something he explained in his own words: *"How can I tell them I am feeling worried because I prefer to be alone, without them saying I'm overreacting. If I tell them I'm worried because I like to be alone... their solution will be simply to tell me I should go out."*

I intervened there pointing to what he said, in a simple and direct way: *"It's not that preference that worries you."*

Nick got emotional and recognized that: *"No, I am used to being alone... what worries me is what I've told you, that I started thinking 'What happens if this get worse?' and then I started feeling that it could indeed happen. If it remains at this level, okay, I'm just different from my family, different from most people my age... that doesn't bother me, I have always been different from the rest, lonelier, I prefer to do things I can do by myself, I don't like team sports, I don't like to work in groups..."*

Frightened about the possibility that his natural tendency to be alone might get worse, Nick again tried to seek shelter in examples about his preference, again trying to believe or make me believe that what was going on was the same as ever.

However, in psychotherapy we wouldn't lessen the importance of what was happening. Nick had too much of that at home. I returned to the point, telling him: *"It seems that what worries you is that something is changing."*

"Yes... something is changing," he recognized, but immediately he downplayed it: *"It's a small change, maybe I am making it worse imagining what would happen if it gets worse."*

As you can imagine, I disregarded the second part, and I continued the dialogue with that part of him that was worried and anxious about what was happening to him. *"What changes have you felt?"*

"I have noticed something when I'm with my girlfriend. Now, after just a couple of hours of being together, I say to her that I'm going home, or take her home... because yeah, I like to be with her, but I also like being alone. Before I needed it less, and I was less forward with her about it, too. The current state doesn't frighten me in itself, it's the tendency that worries me. I get anxious thinking that I will isolate myself from everyone, that finally I will say goodbye, everyone can go to hell, and I will be alone, quietly alone."

In that statement appeared clearly again what worried him. If what was going on was not just his tendency, if something else was going on, his fantasy was that he could end up completely isolated, something that frightened him. It was key to attend to that fear, exactly what he avoided, so we could face what scared him. To give it room to exist, and then to confront it together.

I intervened like this: *"How would your life be, if this would be a tendency that in fact gets worse?"* The goal was to get him to put into words that fantasy that lingered as a threat.

We kept working like this session after session, putting into words that sticky loneliness that frightened him. Thus, Nick started to speak more and more about the changes he felt, about why they scared him, and the causes he thought could be provoking them. Above all, he had a space to talk about his loneliness.

Since the treatment went on like this for a couple of months, instead of sharing every session that followed in detail, I would like to highlight two features of our work for you.

First, something he told me when the treatment was pretty advanced that showed the risk we went through in the first sessions: *"I have to confess that if you would have downplayed my stuff like my family do, I think I would have killed myself... I haven't told you but you were the third therapist I had tried to have therapy with."* As you can see, by giving room to his fears, helping him talk about them, and not downplaying them as the rest of the world had, I allowed him to confront his fears in his own words and eliminate them from his life.

The second thing is how the case ended. Nick kept his natural tendency towards solitude, preferring to watch movies rather than go out. However, he could do it with a peace of mind, without feeling that what he was doing was wrong or that he had to explain himself because he was able to free himself from that sticky loneliness he felt. How? He expressed it like this during one of the last sessions: *"I think it had me trapped because I turned my back on it, but once I faced it, everything was alright."*

His statement showed that Nick stopped avoiding the possibility that what was happening to him was something other than his natural tendency. With the help of psychotherapy, he was brave enough to face the negative changes he was going through, and able to handle a situation that was overwhelming him.

Without a doubt, this case distinctly shows the fundamental difference between ignoring our subjective position and assuming it. Above all, how that produces a therapeutic effect. In the shadows of what we don't accept of ourselves —that is, the unconscious— our fears will only grow and we are not going to be able to do anything about them.

Assuming our subjective position and opening our eyes while standing in that vantage point to see what lurks in what we don't want to see will allow us to name our fears, transforming the unknown terrors into identified fears, named objects that can be acknowledged and understood.

Once they become words, part of our recognized symbolic world, these fears can be defeated by the same words that brought them into the light and make them real. This is why psychotherapy, even if it's 'just words', can help people change.

Sometimes, that is all that is needed.

VII. When Passion Ends

When I work in couples' therapy, I always remember the words of Milton Erickson: "every artichoke has those petals that are discarded. The only way you can enjoy the artichoke is by heaping up the discard, and ignoring it. Being grateful for that nice delightful, delicious, soft, base of the petal."[1]

Most couples, however, come to therapy with the desire to change their partner, sometimes in several different ways, even insisting that they have the right to ask for those changes. Instead of focusing on the good parts, they choose to highlight what is wrong with them.

One of the issues with starting from this point is that if they have the right to change the other person, then their partner has that same right. We thus quickly arrive at a draw, and no one wants to live in an eternal stalemate. In many cases, this stalemate can be resolved if the situation is made clear. Successful therapy, therefore, can start with, and sometimes only needs to consist of, a space to explore both the reasons behind the desire to change the partner and the reasonable limits to those desired changes.

Unfortunately, sometimes the problem that brings them to therapy is truly the heart of the artichoke, and in those cases we cannot simply ignore the problem if we want the couple to continue together. How are we to foster a change in the relationship dynamics when this is the case?

I think it is useful to explain this process through a case where the main issue lies in the couple's sex life, since it's not only a core part of the vast majority of romantic relationships but also an area in which many couples face problems in their lives together.

This case explores what can be done to help save a relationship once the passion is gone. Fortunately in the vast majority of cases, it is possible to reawaken the passion that the partners felt for each other at the beginning of their relationship.

It is worth mentioning, since we are talking about sexual problems, that there are cases in which there don't seem to be any psychological issue that would explain the specific problem the couple is facing. It's always a good idea, especially in those cases, to have a doctor check the hormone levels of both partners, since certain imbalances in thyroid function or testosterone, for example, can produce changes in the sexual desire and performance.

Getting back to my work, I will share with you the case of Carol and David, a married couple that had been together for five years when they came to see me. In the first session they told me they came to therapy because they were arguing a lot, *"always over silly stuff."*

At my inquiry into what *"silly stuff"* meant, they said they had different opinions regarding: the raising of the children, preferences in meals and hobbies, which countries to visit on their holidays, even about the amount of time each of them spent in the bathroom.

It's important to be patient with this kind of wandering in the first sessions, since the key of the case could be found in even seemingly innocent statements. It's also true that patients sometimes need to talk about other things, and not the real issue for which they decided to seek treatment, as a sort of social introduction. They will wait to reveal what's really bothering them when they feel they can trust the therapist. Additionally, taking into account the phenomenon of resistance I explained in the first chapter, if we are impatient as therapists and go directly to the critical point, we could trigger a closure in their discourse.

After allowing Carol and David to list all of the *"silly stuff"*, they both reached a point where they told me they agreed that their main problem was the lack of sexual intercourse. Weeks could pass without them having sex, and they were so tired of this being an issue that they were even questioning the continuation of their relationship.

Each of them had their own theory about this problem. David told me that he was tired of initiating sex because, in the last year, Carol almost never allowed anything to happen. Carol didn't deny her rejection of her husband, but she explained that for her the problem is that he *"cut to the chase"* and that she needed him to be romantic, to take his time, like when she was *"his girlfriend"*. David interrupted her to clarify that he had no desire to be romantic because of the constant rejection, saying he was frustrated and did not have the energy for any kind of foreplay.

As you can see, we were in the midst of a vicious circle. What would be the optimal result in this case? Without a doubt, that each partner wanted again to have sexual intercourse with the other, in a manner and frequency they could both enjoy.

Wouldn't it be easy to just tell them to break the vicious circle? To tell David to treat her as his girlfriend? To tell Carol to accept his advances? It would indeed be the simplest thing to say, but human beings are not known for their obedience. We have already discussed the phenomenon of resistance and, besides this unconscious phenomenon, our pride make us often prefer that the other party is the one that yields.

What could I do then? I had to find a way to work around to the issue from a less-than direct approach. I, therefore, proposed the following prescription: *"Until the session next week, every night you have to cuddle, hug each other, kiss each other, everything that Carol wants, but you are not allowed to have sexual intercourse, even if both of you want to."*

Why was this intervention useful? The key is that it was a trap.

If David followed my prescription, the vicious circle would be broken. He was not allowed to cut to the chase and would behave romantically, like when Carol was his girlfriend, and thus the reason of Carol's rejection of his advances would be gone, at least temporarily. And if she didn't want to have sexual intercourse with him after he had been romantic, she was not going to be the one rejecting him, since she would only be following my prescription, and thus would also be breaking the vicious circle from the other side.

If the couple didn't fulfill what was prescribed, and after their cuddle they did have sex, the vicious circle would also have been broken, since they would have had sex after David behaved romantically (as Carol wanted) without her rejecting his advances (as David feared).

Erickson recommended this paradoxical approach sometimes, in which we, as therapists, suggest something with the hidden goal of our patients doing exactly the opposite —whether because of the absurdity of our suggestion, or because of their unconscious resistance— thus producing a change in their behavior that unlocks the situation.

An excellent example of this, useful both in therapy and outside of it, is an intervention that Erickson used to make before the couple started to criticize each other and to demand the other should change. He used to suggest to them something like this: *"While we are at this, I suppose both of you want to leave aside all the positive elements of each other for now."*

Do you see the trap? If they say no, that they don't want to leave the positive elements aside, they are accepting that they do exist. If they say yes, that they do want to leave the positive elements aside for now... they also accept they exist.

Another example of this technique, in this case one whose effect would appear after the session, is an intervention made by Erickson with a couple that argued all day. He told them that they had to argue every day, at a determined time, but not outside that time. Obviously, it was hard to look at the clock and start fighting in such a scheduled way —since arguments are emotional and spontaneous most of the time— so the couple didn't fight when they were allowed. Sometimes they even laughed because of the absurdity of the situation.

What happened with David and Carol? When they came to my office the following week they had been romantic and loving to one and other, but they had not had sex. As you can see, the intervention had worked in a direct way, if not in the paradoxical manner I would have preferred. Carol was happy, because she had been thinking that David didn't love her anymore, and that because of that he was not romantic. *"I felt like I used to feel,"* Carol would repeat smiling many times in that session.

David was looking forward to what I was going to say. As he expected, I told them that the coming week they should do the opposite, that is, that David was going to cut to the chase and that Carol would see if she accepted him or not, knowing now that her husband still loved her.

This time I was sure he was not going to follow my direction, that he would instead be as romantic as the week before. Why was I so sure of this? The reason David gave for not being romantic and tender with his wife was his fear of rejection, and I suspected that now that she was less likely to reject him, because of the reassurance she received from his romantic gestures in the previous assignment, he would naturally still want to behave romantically.

They came to the third session apologizing, since they had not followed the assignment I had given them. David considered that it would have been unkind and unnatural to just cut to the chase, so they engaged in a little foreplay when they had sex that week —each of the three times.

I asked them how they felt about the last two weeks and both replied that they were happy with the results. David recognized it was impossible for his wife to accept his advances every time, and that of course cutting to the chase was not the best way to get her to accept him. *"Women are different from men, and there's nothing to do about it,"* he said with a smile. Carol was happy because she felt loved again, instead of being *"just a piece of meat,"* and she also recognized that rejecting sex for so long had not been healthy either.

About their fights over *"silly stuff"* that supposedly were the reason that brought them to my office, both of them were surprised that they had almost forgotten about all of it, since they had stopped arguing about those things once the issues around sex had been resolved. Without a doubt, those topics were petals to be discarded.

When I saw them again a couple of weeks later, they were still doing fine and their treatment was happily ended.

There are cases, however, in which one of the members of the couple decides to not continue the relationship. This is a decision that can be hard to accept, since it involves painful consequences for both of them, not to mention any children they may have. It is important that therapists working with couples never forget that, even after going to therapy and listening to each other calmly and clearly for the first time, some individuals still find that they cannot continue with their relationship.

There are a lot of situations that could provoke something like this to happen. I will use as an example a case of economic dependency that had all the features of an abusive relationship, but seemed normal for them before they came to see me.

I must clarify first that there is nothing inherently wrong with one partner supporting the other financially. There are hundreds of situations in which this must be the case, and plenty of them are respectable and compatible with a couple's happiness. There are other times, however, when the situation becomes abusive or, as we will see in this case, when money becomes the only reason to still be with each other.

Emily and Brian were both twenty-five years old when they came to my office, and had been together for seven years. They met in their first year of university studying civil engineering, and a few months later they were dating.

They came to the office at Emily's request, as she was tired of the constant arguing between them. When I asked them about the cause of their quarrels, Brian told me that he was frustrated that she didn't have time to go out with him like before, and that the frequency of their sexual intercourse had decreased considerably. *"The problem is that she has become this bitter old hag,"* said Brian.

Emily, tired and sad, told me she didn't know what to do. She explained that she did have the desire to go out with her boyfriend, but that she was always exhausted; she felt guilty because she knew she was not behaving like most woman her age.

During that first session, their current situation became clear to me. When Emily graduated Brian had still one semester left, because he had failed some classes, but they decided to leave their parents' homes and live together. Their thinking was that, for one semester, Emily could handle the expenses alone. This plan did not work out, however, as this situation did not change for the next two years. Brian had still not gotten his degree when they came to my office. The situation had turned critical the year before when Brian's parents stopped paying for his tuition because they thought he was not taking it seriously and they had already paid for an extra year because of his irresponsibility. Brian considered leaving school and pursuing other interests, but Emily insisted she could work to pay for his tuition. Emily explained to me that she didn't want him to sacrifice his dreams just because of money.

Emily then started to work extra hours, to be able to pay for the expenses of the house and Brian's university. She left home at seven in the morning, and returned around ten in the evening. She didn't have time for anything else, something that Brian complained about constantly. Whenever he told her that they should go out for a couple of drinks, Emily replied that she preferred to sleep, a response that always made him furious.

The latest argument between them, and the reason why Emily finally decided to seek treatment, was about Brian's school holidays. Emily asked Brian if he was thinking of taking some of that free time to work and help her with the expenses. He angrily replied that he deserved to rest. *"Doesn't she understand that I need to rest to be able to get grades good enough to graduate?"* he asked me in that first session.

Is he taking advantage of Emily? Is the situation acceptable? Is it right? Those are questions that involve the opinion and moral code of each person, thus a psychotherapist shouldn't consider them for their intervention.

Therapy can, however, clarify the situation, discussing the intentions and responsibilities of each member of the couple. Sometimes that is enough to produce a change in the way they understand the situation, or even to make different choices. Returning to the idea mentioned in the first chapter, we try to reveal the subjective position of each partner, both to themselves and to one another.

I invited Brian to imagine a hypothetical situation: *"If you were paying for your expenses, including your education, what would you do during the holidays?"* Without any hesitation he replied: *"Obviously I would work. I wouldn't have a choice."*

Emily was shocked with the answer. They continued talking and I tried to help Brian be more empathetic towards the position of his girlfriend. After all, he considered it reasonable to work in the situation I had asked him to imagine, so why was it unreasonable for Emily to ask him to work during his holidays?

Brian said, however, that since Emily earned enough money to cover their expenses, it would be unfair and *"really mean of her"* not to pay for his education. I tried to move the dialogue towards what they did agreed on, that is, that they spent little time together and what time they did have was of *"low quality"*. Emily said that, for the sake of their relationship, she would prefer to stop paying for his university so that she could return home earlier and they could have more time together.

Brian said that he wouldn't accept something like that, and that he would end the relationship if she did that, since partners were supposed to help one another during difficult times. Emily, crying, told him that she would pay for everything else, that he would only have to pay for his tuition, pointing out that he could take out a loan to cover the costs. Brian kept saying over and over again that she was betraying him.

Emily asked to have an individual session the day after this session with Brian. She didn't know what to think, *"Am I wrong? Am I being unfair?"* she asked. Without me saying anything, she arrived at the idea that maybe Brian was with her because of her money. She said, *"it's ugly even to think about it,"* but she couldn't get it out of her head.

This session helped her to realize she really wanted to stop working extra hours so that she would be able to spend more time doing *"couple's stuff"* with Brian. If the root of their problems was indeed their lack of time together, she reasoned, there was no other solution.

The following week, in their second session together, Emily told me that she had suggested Brian take out a loan just for the last semester. He had felt betrayed but had finally accepted. After that decision, however, Emily had come home early every day of the week and invited him out but he refused each time. She also tried to initiate sex and this time he was the one who was tired.

The next session she came alone, telling me Brian felt angry because of the *"betrayal"* and didn't want to come. She explained that the same thing as the week before had happened, with different excuses but always with the same outcome: Emily invited him out, tried to talk to him or initiate sex, and Brian would not accept.

She came alone again next time, and told me she had decided to break up with Brian. Emily had reached the conclusion that he had been with her, at least during the last year, only because of her financial support. In the individual therapy that we continued after the breakup she asked herself many times how could she have not seen something so obvious, and said she wanted to work on herself to prevent it from happening ever again.

As you can see, what we search for —even in couple's therapy— is not a fixed outcome, but the reveal of the subjective position of our patients. With this information we can then offer a deeper understanding into what is 'really' going on. With new clarity, most couples solve their problems. Others, sadly, find them unsolvable.

As a therapist, we are not there to choose the path they walk, we are only there to help shed light upon it.

---

1. Erickson, Milton. Conversations with Milton H. Erickson, M.D. (Book 2). Triangle Press, 1999.

VIII. INFIDELITY AS A TRAUMA

One of the most common reasons for couples to seek therapy is dealing with infidelity. The individual that cheated generally comes full of guilt and promising to never do it again, while their partner most times is unsure about the possibility of continuing together, because it seems impossible that their trust can be recovered.

In this chapter I will try to explain the tragedy of infidelity, focusing on the victim, since most psychotherapists writing on the topic have written about the cheating partner and the reasons behind their actions. I will also explain the effects cheating has on a person through the theory of trauma. Finally, I will show some steps to follow at home, and in therapy, that facilitate overcoming the pain and anger produced by being cheated on and, however slowly, begin the process of forgiveness and attempt to rebuild trust.

Before turning to the victim's experience I want to share a few words about the cheating partner. There is no single explanation about why a person is unfaithful. There are cases where there is a psychological or psychiatric disorder at the root of infidelity, but that is in a minority of situations. In some cases it is the consequence of not loving the partner anymore, but there are also people who cheat on a dearly beloved partner. The common assumption that *"if they cheated on me, they don't love me anymore"*, is thus not applicable to all the cases, so the actual cause in a specific case has to be explored, a process which can benefit from the support of therapy.

Even if the partners both still love each other, however, the commitment made at the beginning of the relationship may be breached if they had agreed to be monogamous, alongside any other implicit and explicit agreements made on the outset of their relationship.

It is the breach in what we expected that I will focus on when discussing infidelity, and the effects it can have on the partner who did not cheat. What happens to a person who finds out their partner cheated on them? If we center our attention there, we will find much more similarity between them than we would between the people that cheat on their partners. Because of what cheating means, and the typical reactions people have when they find out about it, we can say that the victim of an unfaithful partner is indeed suffering from a traumatic event.

What is trauma? A traumatic event refers to an experience that goes beyond the capacity that a person has to handle it. They find themselves unable to integrate the ideas and emotions that the event provokes with the rest of their life. In psychological terms, it generally occurs when there is a strong incongruence between what has happened and what the person thought about their life and their future, resulting in a state of profound confusion and uncertainty. When a person is cheated on, it's not unusual to hear them say: *"I never would have thought they would have done something like this"*, a clear indication of the unexpected and unfathomable nature of infidelity.

It's useful to understand that when we talk about trauma, we talk about a breach, an experience that breaks the continuity of our story in a sudden way, marking a before and after in our lives. After a discontinuity such as this happens in our story, certain characteristic phenomena start to occur. Recognizing these as symptoms of a trauma helps both the victim and the person who cheated to understand the behaviors as something to expect in the journey through trauma.

Past   Present   Future

The first symptom is that the memory of the traumatized person can be affected in different ways. It is common for them to constantly remember the fact and think about it, trying again and again to find any sense in it, to find an explanation; many victims experience a desperate search for meaning, hoping to be able to restore the continuity in their lives by pinpointing the cause of the disruption. Here the constant question *"Why?"* will be repeated, especially to their partner, needing an answer time and time again, even if it is always the same answer they are given.

Another symptom, a product of the breach shown in the previous figure, is a certain degree of amnesia or difficulty in remembering aspects of the relationship previous to the trauma. Since there is now a discontinuity in the story, it's hard to traverse the memories to moments prior to the infidelity. The person is in this way stuck in the trauma, only able to remember and think about what happened there.

Even when the therapeutic process is working, even when the person is able to forgive and trust again, flashbacks can occur. This means that sometimes images of the traumatic event will appear unexpectedly, especially if something related to it triggered those memories. Common triggers in these cases could be hearing the name of the partner's lover, walking past the place where they found out about the deed, or even dreaming about it. The image doesn't come alone; sadly it also brings back all the emotionality, all the pain, that appeared at the moment the traumatic event happened. It's important to know that flashbacks are a normal part of the path, that they are even expected. This allows both members of the relationship to not see this as an absolute setback, or that all of their efforts have been useless, but to understand it as a part of the healing process.

Another characteristic symptom of a trauma is a simplified emotional response, in which anger and sadness appear suddenly, apparently without explanation. We can understand this from a biological level: if an organism is threatened, a quick response is preferable and, in fact, more adaptive. For the victim of infidelity, their partner was, or still is, the enemy that threatened their sense of safety and continuity, and it is to be expected they will show less tolerance and more irritability towards that threat.

It's not unusual to find dichotomous emotionality in victims of infidelity, that is, feeling either all good or all bad. The past of the relationship, long before the infidelity, is sometimes seen as a happy and almost perfect period where no problems existed. The future, on the other hand, is seen as a barren wasteland devoid of trust and love. Once we are able to recover the continuity of our story, to give meaning to what happened —not to justify the deed but to understand it— we can connect that past with that future, breaking down the black-and-white dichotomy in remembering the negative moments that could have precipitated or warned of the infidelity, and believing there is some hope to trust again in the future.

Now that we understand why being cheated on is a trauma, we can discuss what to do about it.

First, it is important that both partners are in agreement with what they will refer to with the word 'infidelity'. It is always helpful to define terms in relation to behaviors, that is, to things we can all perceive. In this way the presence of that phenomenon can be evaluated in an objective way, more or less.

For example: it is one thing to say that the problem is that the partner is an alcoholic, but it is quite a different story to say that there is a problem because every time they go out together he or she drinks until they get drunk. One definition is arguable, almost an insult, while the second one is possible to evaluate objectively. *"Are you an alcoholic?"* is a very different question *than "Did you get drunk last Saturday?"*

A good definition of infidelity must, of course, include sexual acts with a person outside the relationship, unless it is an open relationship in which an explicit agreement has been made that allowed extra relationship sexual conduct. The definition should not, however, end there. It is also important to clarify all the non-sexual conduct that either member of the couple considers to also breach their relationship agreement such as: sharing intimate pictures or even feelings with another person, spending more time with another person than with the partner, or any other situation one of the partners considers relevant.

I remember a case that illustrates this point very well. The wife felt her husband had been unfaithful because, during the important times in her life, such as her father's funeral or the birth of their daughter, her husband had not been with her. Instead, he had been supporting his best friend, a woman that he had met at work, who was sad at those times for unrelated reasons.

The husband recognized he had not been there for his wife, but he explained that while his wife had been accompanied by her family, his friend had been alone so he thought his presence had been more helpful at her side. He disagreed that his behavior had amounted to being unfaithful. For him, and there was no way for his wife to dissuade him, infidelity meant to have sex with another person, and nothing less than that.

The argument between them had centered on semantics, the meaning of the word itself, leaving aside what was more important to discuss: the facts of what had happened between them. I proposed they not refer to what had happen as 'infidelity', since there was no agreement about its meaning, but to use the term 'disloyalty' instead. The husband was not sure about this new word, but he was open to discuss it and to the possibility of calling his behavior disloyal.

As you can see, since we were going to focus our attention on actions, the specific word we use to refer to them was not important. Thus, we can avoid the obstacle of someone not recognizing that their behavior was unfaithful just by changing the word with which we will work. As I have tried to explain in this book, in therapy the important part of the words we use is the position they reveal, more than the actual words themselves.

Once in agreement of the words we will use for the issue at hand, we can decide with the couple on the goals of the therapy.

What changes would they like to see once the treatment is over? What kind of couple would they like to be in the future? These questions put forgiveness and the overcoming of trauma on the horizon, and at the same time allow for other desired changes to appear in the discussion of desire outcomes or goals. In answering these questions, the couple will also reveal much about the story of the relationship. And, in doing that, we can start to contextualize the infidelity, or disloyalty, within the relationship, instead of seeing it as an event outside of it.

A good example of the importance of goal setting is the issue of going out. If a person that had an affair tells their partner that in part they cheated on them because they never went out together, the most probable outcome will be anger in the victim, thinking their partner is trying to justify their action.

However, if the same person instead tells their partner that they miss going out with them and that in the future they would like to go out together more often, it becomes less a justification and more a positive goal to improve the relationship, and most of the time is seen as such by the victim.

There are some long-term goals that are always a good idea to talk about, especially when working with couples that have gone through an affair. First, there has to be an agreement about the emotional and social boundaries with other people. Second, that both parties will make an effort to rebuild the relationship, trying to the best of their abilities to satisfy the emotional and physical needs of their partner.

We then have to think of short-term goals that, through their fulfillment bring the couple closer to the achievement of their designated long-term goals. Since we have established infidelity is a trauma, and that talking about it is the only way to overcome it, one of the goals should often be being able to talk about the deed in a clear but respectful way. Often doubts will remain and questions will be repeated, so we will have to help the cheating partner to be patient and tolerate this stage. It is the only way for their partner to achieve some kind of meaning or sense behind what happened, and thus be able to connect it with their story and their present, restoring its continuity.

It is helpful to remind the couple of the typical reactions to trauma while they are attempting this, to help them to empathize with the hurt partner, and not think the repetitions are caused by cruelty or even other mental health issues.

In the same spirit of finding a meaning behind the infidelity, it is good to talk about the elements, both within and external to their relationship, that they believe contributed to the infidelity. It's not important to arrive at one clear cause that explains what happened, but the simple fact of talking and exploring different hypotheses is useful to make sense and connect the trauma with the rest of both their lives. If the father of the cheating partner had an affair in the past it doesn't explain anything by itself but it starts to give the deed a context. This knowledge connects their behavior with the past and stops it from being an isolated event that, exactly because of that rupture with the rest of their lives, would be impossible to assimilate.

It's also useful to talk about the condition of the relationship before the infidelity happened, to be able to recover bit by bit that past, which can be lost or distorted in the memory by the trauma.

Once the facts are clear enough, including the details needed by the hurt partner, alongside the probable causes and the condition of the relationship when the affair occurred, it is possible to begin to identify the behavioral changes, of both partners, that could help to avoid a future infidelity and improve the relationship at the same time.

Finally, it is important that the victim of the infidelity understands forgiveness as a process, and not a clear cut event. This means that forgiveness can ebb and flow, sometimes more and sometimes less, but that doesn't mean that they are taking it back or 'un-forgiving' their partner. It's a gradual, and not always straight, path.

People often think that it will be impossible to forgive something, because they think forgiveness means to forget, or to forgive one hundred percent. When we understand forgiveness as a journey, where every step counts, where backtracking is natural, it is possible to see forgiveness as something achievable, even if it is only at ninety percent. This gradient is an important distinction for couples to understand as a relationship where there is ninety percent forgiveness is radically different to one where there is no forgiveness and, in fact, it is very similar to one where there is total forgiveness. Sometimes ninety percent is the closest they may be able to get to a goal that can be ultimately unachievable after an event as traumatic as infidelity.

In this way, the therapeutic process can work on one hand in the healing of trauma —by helping to tolerate being stuck at that point in time and slowly connecting it with the rest of the story of their relationship in order to become unstuck— while on the other hand it can also help by opening new ways in which the couple can become stronger and, in some cases, have an even better relationship in the future through open discussion and the setting of goals.

If we want to relate this to what we discussed about our focus on the subjective position of our patients, and the shift of it as the trigger for their change, we can say that trauma produces a limited perspective of our own story, censoring or blocking some of the chapters. In the case of infidelity, if the couple is to stay together we have to be able to shift the position to incorporate the deed and, at the same time, to explore the perspective of the future in order to decide if it is one in which they want to stay together as a couple.

In summary, understanding infidelity as a trauma allows both the couple and the professional to focus enough time on the deed itself, before looking to the past in search of a cause, or to the future that may seem barren after such a painful event.

In addition, trauma theory explains the phenomena of memory changes and the emotions present in this kind of case, while also explaining why they are a natural reaction to this type of event. This work can open the door to a not so distant future where the infidelity is included as a dark time of the couple's story, a story that may still continue with the couple choosing to stay together, possibly in a relationship that is even stronger than before.

IX. RAISING A TEENAGER

Being a parent is not an easy thing, and many agree that it becomes harder when the children are going through adolescence. However, with some simple techniques — derived from hundreds of studies about human behavior— it is possible to make this challenge easier.

I would like to begin by telling you of a case recounted by Jay Haley in *The Art of Strategic Therapy*, since it's a good way to synthesize the spirit of this chapter.

A social worker was in charge of a kid that set things on fire. He did it not only at home or school, but he walked from one place to the other throwing lit matches into the garbage bins on the sidewalk. The diagnosis seemed easy: pyromaniac.

The professional complained at her workplace that she did not know what to do with a pyromaniac, and that she needed the support of the psychologists and psychiatrist. There was a clinical meeting in which the director of the center, after hearing about the case, said that it was obviously an 'oedipal problem' and he promptly stood up, finishing the meeting. The social worker remained seated crying, because she had not received any suggestion or help regarding how to work with this child.

When a psychotherapist saw her crying, he asked her what was going on. After she explained, he said: "Well, to set something on fire you need to have matches." He told her to give the kid a penny for each unburnt match that he gave her. "Can I do that?" she asked, incredulous.

Willing to do anything, she talked with the parents and with their help she put the plan in motion. The kid was happy to get the money, and the parents were glad to get the first concrete help. In a short time, the kid stopped lighting fires.

This is then the spirit of this chapter, that is, how fast techniques or tactics, even if they don't solve all the problems underlying what we face in psychotherapy, without a doubt can help to produce a quick relief in some cases. Behavior changes that, in some situations, allows us to clear the way for a deeper transformation such as the change in the subjective position that we have reviewed in the previous chapters.

As an example I will use the case of Mark, a fourteen year-old patient. His parents came to my office because they felt that lately their son *"has become rebellious, he has changed,"* and this made them worry about his future.

When I asked them about the changes, they told me that until the previous year Mark fulfilled his obligations without issue: he made his bed, cleaned his room, studied enough to have good grades, etc. When he turned fourteen, however, all of that had stopped. When they asked him to do something, he answered in a rude way, ending the conversation with *"I don't think so."* Confronted with this, his father had almost hit him more than once and only the mother, begging her husband to show more patience, had been able to prevent physical violence.

It was clear what the issue was for the parents but before proposing any solution, I had to ask how Mark's parents had already tried to make him do his chores. One of the ways they had tried to gain some kind of control over their son's behavior was through controlling his money.

It's not a bad idea to use money as a reward because it grants autonomy to the young and is, thus, very important to them. However, it is important to know how to use it properly. Since the problems with Mark had begun, his parents had decided to withhold his allowance each time he didn't fulfill his responsibilities. When he got a bad grade, for example, they would say to him that he was not going to get any money that week. The problem is that they would give the allowance sooner or later, either because he needed the money to buy his lunch or pay for the bus to school, or because his mother thought that the punishment was too harsh. Mark's father commented that this was another problem they had, a difference in how they thought they should raise their son, and that he was *"annoyed that I am overruled in my house."*

Any solution I was going to propose, therefore, had to also take care of this issue, promoting a previously determined explicit agreement between the two parents so that their child raising approaches were aligned. This alignment was crucial to the success of any intervention.

What Mark's parents were doing, by removing something positive as the allowance, can be considered a punishment. Hundreds of behavioral studies have been made about this type of punishment-based approach, showing two main problems with it. First, to be at all effective, each time the behavior we want to eliminate occurs the punishment has to follow immediately. Second, and more importantly, punishment has been found to not be the most effective mechanism to create behavioral change.

If punishment is not effective, what is the best way to change behavior, according to the behaviorist research? The answer is, through reinforcement. That is, to give something positive to the person —or to remove something negative— after the behavior we wish to see occurs. Common examples of reinforcement include: giving a prize to the child when they get good grades, or after being denied the chance to go to a party, let him go because he behaved well for a whole week. The example by Haley that I gave at the beginning of this chapter is a perfect example of positive reinforcement being used to help the child stop lighting matches.

A particular behavior Mark's parents had a problem with was him not taking out the trash. They didn't know what to do to make their son do something as simple as this chore and they used it as an example over and over again to show how severe the situation was, repeating often *"he doesn't even take out the trash."*

Once the situation with the parents was clear, I proposed to them that before planning any kind of intervention, I should see their son first, to form my own opinion about the issue. I wanted to see if the behavior Mark's parents had told me about could have other causes —for example the presence of potential mental health disorders or drug use— to determine if the issue was more complicated than simple puberty and the behavioral changes it carries.

Fortunately, after seeing Mark twice, I was pretty certain that there were not any problems besides the typical ones that come with his age, generated by the tension between autonomy and obedience. Mark told me that he was *"tired of my parents giving and taking my allowance all the time"*, and that he would *"almost prefer to not get any money if they will be blackmailing me with it."* About the changes in his behavior, he agreed that he was doing fewer chores around the house but said it was because high school demanded more of his time to study.

We then made a plan with the parents in the following sessions that involved both their expectations and Mark's. I proposed to have a minimum allowance that would be given to him no matter what. The amount would be less than what they could potentially give him, but enough to cover his lunches and the bus to and from school. Once this amount was stipulated, we made a schedule in which Mark had one chore per day such as taking out the trash, making his bed, or other domestic tasks his parents wanted him to do. It was important that it was just one chore, to respect his complaint about the time it took him to study.

Each day, if he had done the chore, they would mark a circle on the calendar but if he didn't do it, they would mark a cross. When he achieved three circles in a week, Mark would get a bonus in his allowance, an amount agreed upon by him and his parents beforehand.

I explained to his mother that she had to respect the agreement we were making, and that if she gave her son money under the table she would sabotage our attempt.

Before starting with the schedule, I asked them to come to a session with Mark to review together the calendar plan, or as the father humorously called it, *"the mission."*

Once we made some adjustments to get an agreement on all parts, I asked them to put the schedule in a place visible to everyone, to avoid having the parents reminding Mark constantly about his chores, something he already said he hated.

After a few weeks the three of them had grown used to this new system. Mark was happy to be certain of a fixed amount of allowance and he felt more in control of his own actions. *"If I am too exhausted one day, I simply don't do what I had to do that day... I know what that cross means, but I have other days to fix it,"* he explained in one of the following sessions. His parents were also happy because they hadn't enjoyed having to nag him about his chores, not to mention having to punish him so often. The new system, thus, seemed perfect for the entire family. Mark's father was also glad to not feel constantly undermined, stating that now there was *"a written law"* that supported his decisions regarding how to handle Mark's behavior.

It is important to note that the intervention was based on their ideas, because interventions that are created taking into account the patients' thoughts and proposals have a greater chance of both immediate success and to remain in place once the therapy is over.

This is just one among a lot of techniques that can help us with the typical behavioral situations that arise in adolescence. The important thing for a therapist is to know a variety of techniques and to apply them appropriately. For that, it's not only important to have a theoretical knowledge about the techniques themselves, but also to understand what is important to each individual teenage patient and thus know which stimulus, which reinforcement, would be the most useful to produce the desired change. In this way a successful therapist must be strategic in their treatment of adolescents.

With all patients, therapy works best when approached as a singularity, but in particular with adolescents. Respect for the individuality —that is, their own subjective position— of each case has to always be upheld, as only by respecting it will we be able to produce a true change.

X. CHILDREN'S DRAWINGS
AS A MESSAGE TO THE PARENTS

A couple of years ago, a woman wrote me an e-mail asking if I could do something for her son.

She told me that, after having two unsuccessful therapeutic processes, both with a child psychologist and with a psychiatrist, she had decided to try with me. In her e-mail she referred to the future therapy saying, *"the third time is the charm."*

Mary explained briefly in her e-mail that her six year old son Luke was still not able to control his bladder. In her words, the problem was that her son *"peed himself every night."*

As we have seen in previous chapters, our interventions rarely fall directly on the problem itself but try to target the cause of it to stop it at its root. When we work with children, their problems often reflect a pathological environment, usually in the family system.

I decided to call the mother for a first interview so she could explain to me in more detail what was going on with Luke, while also offering me possible insight into the environment in which he lived, both at home and at school. As mentioned in a previous chapter, I hoped that asking her to come alone would help to make her feel free to speak without having to withhold anything out of fear of the child hearing about certain topics.

The first thing Mary said was that, *"Luke is a normal kid,"* then she extensively described all the areas where her son was an average child, from his marks in school to his place in the pediatric growth curve. Everything was absolutely normal. *"But he keeps peeing himself,"* Mary said again, repeating the statement five times during the session.

When I asked her about her relationship with John, her husband and Luke' father, Mary explained that she was a housewife and her husband an important manager in a telecommunications company. They had been married for eight years, and after Luke was born they decided not to have more children because of ongoing marital problems.

We must not forget that we are trying to find a cause for Luke's problem, the subjective position from which his behavior emerged. It is because of this goal that, without any hesitation I could keep asking about the relationship of his parents even though they were not technically seeking my help as patients themselves.

Mary told me then that besides the typical problems of a married couple, the main issue they had was that she was very jealous, *"almost pathological,"* she said. When I tried to ask her to expand on this statement, she started crying and, after letting me know that what would follow didn't have anything to do with Luke, she told me that some months before she got married she tried to take her own life with pills. The reason? She had the feeling that John was cheating on her.

By the end of the session Mary returned her focus to Luke again saying, *"Fortunately, he is just a kid and doesn't realize anything."* I found this statement particularly notable in light of everything else she had disclosed about her past with Luke's father.

After letting her talk about her fears until she was feeling a bit of relief, I told her that I'd like to see her along with Luke the following week. My primary goal of seeing the child was to see if the cause of the urination issues could be that he was affected by the strained relationship between his parents, but I would also open myself up to other hypotheses if that one didn't match what I encountered.

Mary asked if I wanted her to be in the session. If not, she wanted to go to the mall while Luke was with me. When I told her that the idea was to speak with both of them, she mentioned that it seemed odd to her since the other psychologist used to be alone with Luke in their previous sessions. I just smiled at her and told her that I would see both of them the following week.

In the second session Mary came with Luke, who didn't want to talk, something not unusual in small children. I asked Mary to tell me her son's daily routine with as much detail as she could and I told him not to worry about speaking, that it was not needed for the time being. I offered him a notebook and some colored pencils and crayons, and when he asked me what to draw, I said he could draw whatever wanted.

Why did I ask to hear about his routine? To be sure that Mary would not say anything that worried or hurt her son so that he could focus as much as possible on his drawings, since his mother would be telling me things he already knew.

When I saw him more relaxed and with some drawings already in the notebook, I asked him if he could draw his parents now. I kept talking to Mary until he finished his drawing. I asked him to show it to me: there were two human figures in it, typical simple and childish ones, very colorful, with big smiles and a huge sun with dark sunglasses. Mary smiled at him. Then I asked Luke to draw his parents again, but this time at night. I chose the night as the setting because the mother assumed he didn't know she was fighting with her husband, and I was guessing that it was happening at night when he was thought to be asleep

Luke then grabbed a black crayon and furiously drew over the two figures, covering them with dark stains and clouds. There was very little left of the previous drawing. It seemed that Luke was aware of more than Mary believed, or wanted to believe. I suggested that Mary put the drawing on the refrigerator in their kitchen and I told her to leave it there until the next session. I also asked her to tell her husband to talk to me if he wanted to take it off.

This intervention was intended to question the mother's notion that her child did not realize anything about what was going on between her and her husband. If I was right, at an unconscious level, wetting the bed was a call for attention by Luke, a way to say *"I do realize what's going on between you two"*. And if that was true, making sure the drawing was visible to everyone could keep the message intact while changing the way it was delivered, conveying the same information in a way that was less costly for everyone.

I sent that message to be relayed to her husband because in the first session Mary told me that he was not going to come to my office, as he believed psychologists were frauds and that they only *"wanted to rob people of their hard-earned money."* With this intervention, I respected his unwillingness to come to therapy but communicated to him what his son was telling us in the session in an indirect way.

A week later, Mary came with Luke to my office. *"Instead of peeing himself every night, now he does it every other night... we couldn't be happier"* Mary said to me. I told Luke to draw his parents again and he replied by giving me a smirk. While he drew I asked Mary if she or her husband had any ideas about what could be done to help Luke be more relaxed in his daily life.

The boy once again drew two human figures, happy and with the same sun. When I told him to draw them at night, he carefully grabbed the black crayon and drew some lines between and above them, with very little pressure on the paper. The result was a drawing very similar to the previous one, but with less black on it. I smiled at him, and told Mary to take the other drawing off the refrigerator and put on the new one instead.

Their son was clearly telling them that they were doing something right, but that a bit more effort was still needed. The same child that, according to his mother, didn't realize anything was disrupting the peace at night, was in fact understanding perfectly well the relation between his previous drawing and what I assumed, because of the change in his behavior, was a fewer number of quarrels between his parents.

In the fourth session, one month after seeing Mary for the first time, she came to my office alone with John, who said *"I came because this week Luke didn't pee himself at all... I'm here to understand what happened."*

Is there a better way to get the father that doesn't believe in psychotherapists to attend to a session? He came with an open mind, already questioning what he believed, asking me if he could come to my office. Without a doubt, this way was much better than asking him to come under pressure from his wife.

After speaking for a while about the family and their relationship with each other, I asked Luke's father: *"When does a person pee themselves?"*

John answered right away. *"When someone gets a terrible fright"* and, after a pause, he understood what was going on. *"Luke doesn't go to bed scared anymore."*

I kept seeing Mary and John for a couple more sessions, working on their relationship as a couple, in order to create more harmony at home. A month later, Luke still hadn't wet himself again.

People often think that kids don't understand, or don't realize, what's going on in their homes. Generally, a lot of problems would be a lot easier to solve if we accepted that they do understand and know full well what is happening in their family. Children are subjects as adults are, both have their own subjective positions that determine their reality. Once we grasp what they are experiencing according to that position, then we can produce a change at a faster pace than with adults most of the time.

A couple of months later, John and Mary wrote me again, telling me that Luke had made a new drawing and he had put it on the refrigerator by himself.

He had drawn a videogame console.

XI. How to Deal with Madness?

First of all, I want to clarify that in this chapter I am using the term 'madness' to highlight the colloquial use of the phrase, and others like it, to refer to certain mental disorders. You will understand more of why I chose that particular term once you read this chapter.

Ten years ago I had the chance to work in a treatment center for people diagnosed with psychosis. This institution had been established as a response to a request from the authorities of a municipality located in the capital of Chile. This area had been overloaded by the consequences of this kind of diagnose —difficulty in having a job, for example, and the consequent homelessness— and their own lack of resources to provide care. The municipality asked a well-known Church congregation to address the issue. During the last decade, national government had dramatically reduced the number of psychiatric beds available in our hospitals, leaving individuals in need without access any form of treatment and, in many cases, without anywhere to even live.

The congregation in this area, in response to the request, established a small asylum for patients who were diagnosed with psychotic disorders such as: delusions, hallucinations, disorganized thinking, abnormal motor behavior, and negative symptoms (such as diminished emotional expression and severe lack of motivation to perform life activities), thus helping the neighborhood by addressing the most severe behaviors. There were thirty male patients living in this asylum, aged between thirty and fifty years old.

The conditions were theoretically not bad, at least compared to other asylums. There was a room for each patient, plus a living room and outdoor yard for common use. Unfortunately, the living room door was kept locked and it was only used when one of the staff brought a movie for everyone to watch. The yard was a space of nearly 100 square meters of bare dirt and nothing else. Not even a chair or a table. Not a single thing.

The only office in the asylum, used exclusively by the staff team, had a corner filled with a great number of boxes full of the patients' files. The first thing I did, of course, was to read the files of the current patients.

They contained nothing but diagnoses.

One after the other, each file contained multiple diagnoses, often contradicting each other, that were made by dozens of interns or psychology students who came to do their assignments in this institution, and then left.

The director of the asylum, who was the only psychologist working there, told me that the reason there was nothing written about treatment in the patient files was simple: the only kind of psychological treatment that was carried out in the asylum was the weekly body psychotherapy carried out by her. This treatment approach is a physical rather than verbal modality that involves moving and touching the body. This treatment was offered in addition to a pharmacological-based assessment made by a psychiatrist once a year to assess what medications were to be administered to that patient for the entire year. These two treatment combined —especially with the low frequency that they were administered— do not configure the adequate psychological or psychiatric care at all.

After reading the files, I proceeded to make my own diagnoses for each of the patients. What for? I needed clear diagnoses, free from the contradictions in the files, that would allow me to define what would be useful for the patients, for their benefit, for their dignity. A patient is not interested in knowing what kind of psychosis they are suffering from, if it is not reflected in the treatment they receive. I wanted information about each one of them, what was their opinion about living here, what things did not seem right to them, what changes they would make. I wanted to treat them like any human being deserves to be treated.

After deciding I needed to make these diagnoses, I realized I had to look for a place where I could see the individual patients in order to make them. Even though each patient had a room of his own, they only contained a bed and a bedside table. I finally chose to take one of the chairs from the living room and turn it into 'the therapist's chair', bringing it to the room of the patient I was seeing at that time. After a while the patients were able to perfectly distinguish between the psychotherapeutic context when the chair was in their room and the informal context when we were in the yard or having breakfast.

What did I find out? I think that the first conversation I had with a patient reflects the situation quite well:

Jorge: How about talking for a while?

Patient: Yes, no problem. I like talking, no one here talks with anyone. Sometimes other psychologists come. Are you going to show me some spots or something like that?

J: No, none of that... the idea is just to talk, maybe more than once, so I can get to know you better.

P: Hmm... I'm not someone interesting... my life has become something pretty boring... the only thing I want is to get away from here, I don't want to be here anymore... I don't have any problem talking with you, but if you ask me what I want, I want that, I want to get away from here... every time someone asks me how I'm doing, I say the same thing... I want to get away from here... but nobody listens, nobody does anything...

When I asked him about what he would like to do, he said *"a lot of things... being able to do things with my hands... we can't do anything here... we just lie down in our rooms and that's it. They don't understand that we're still alive, we have faults but we can live, it's not a death sentence..."*

The rest of the first interviews with the patients were practically identical. Everyone was bored and tired of not being able to do anything. However, shortly after I began talking with each one of them every week, they became more active and started to spend a little more time with each other in the yard.

The director told me that it seemed odd to her that they spend time in the yard during the day, instead of being in their rooms. *"Why do they go to the yard if there are not even chairs?"* she said.

I contacted the congregation running the asylum and managed to obtain some secondhand tables and chairs that we put in the yard. I then had the idea of painting a checkerboard on each of their surfaces and giving each patient two sets of checkers to keep in his room so that they were not dependent on staff for access.

When I came back a week after setting up the tables, the staff who worked at the asylum were not so happy with the results.

The patients now spent most of the day in the yard, either playing checkers with each other or talking. Some of them had asked the director for chess pieces, a request that had not yet received an answer. The staff members explained to me that when the patients spent all day long in their rooms, staff worried less about them and could focus on the administrative duties of the asylum instead (cooking, cleaning, etc.). But now that the patients were spending time together, the staff had to watch them all the time, which made their work more difficult.

In response to this position of the staff, the director told me that they would leave the tables and chairs where they were for one more month, since maybe the patients were interested in them simply because they were something new, but she also told me to be less encouraging of interaction and to stop *"causing trouble for the staff."*

After a month, the situation just got *"worse."* The patients kept playing in the yard and talking with each other. The daily meals were not in silence anymore, but with the human noise of conversation. Some of them even told me their ideas about new changes they wanted to see in the asylum. Above everything, they wanted to do more things. They wanted to feel useful. They wanted to feel human.

The staff, however, did not know what other things the patients could do in the asylum without causing more work for them. Finally, after an exhausting meeting between myself and the fulltime staff, they agreed to give the patients a dusting cloth so they could help clean their rooms. You cannot imagine the smiles that this simple right brought to the faces of the patients.

The few relatives who visited the patients were aware of the changes, mostly because of the fact that their relatives now talked with them more easily and pleasantly. It was not like the conversations they could have with other people, but to them the change was significant. The frequency of these family visits increased, and we managed to have them bring movies for the patients to watch.

The lesson I learned from all of this is that the most basic elements of how we treat the people that society had deemed 'mad' —particularly in a treatment center that will house most of the patients for the rest of their lives— is fundamental to their recovery. This may seem obvious to you but, as you can see, in this account there is not a single psychological technique applied, just a little common sense, empathy, and compassion, and yet the intervention resulted in dramatic change in the lives of the individuals.

I would have loved to immediately start applying the treatments of the school where I was trained, meeting the problems of psychosis and facing them with the tools I learned at university. Yes, I would have loved to, because I love my profession. But first I had to just listen to them, trying to grasp their subjective position even amidst these peculiar circumstances.

Unfortunately, this story does not have a happy ending. After maintaining the new setup for a couple of months, the director told me that the asylum could not go on like that. Due to the increased activity of the patients such as interacting in the yard, going to visit each other in the rooms, the presence of relatives, etc. it was necessary to have more staff members on active duty at any given time. She said that there were simply not funds to expand staffing and so they had to make the patients spend more time in their rooms, set a schedule for use of the yard, and limit the frequency of the relatives' visits to the weekend.

In an institution supposedly dedicated to the care and treatment of human beings, basic human needs for socialization and activity were not allowed. It is not clear who is mad, the patients or our society.

XII. The Moment of Concluding

What I have tried to show through reviewing these different cases is that, with the help of psychoanalytic therapy, people do change. The key to fostering this kind of meaningful change is creating a shift in the individual's subjective position. That is what matters. The means and techniques used to produce that change —including those given by the strategic therapy or behaviorist research— are just that, means to the end. What defines these interventions as psychoanalytic is to consider the shift in the subjective position as our goal.

As we saw in the first chapter, it is our own subjective position that determines how we experience what happens to us, what we feel, and what we think. Thus, it is this position that determines the presence of symptoms and the suffering that we try to reduce in therapy.

Even though this individual position defines us as subjects, as the point from which we observe our lives, because it shapes and directs everything we understand about the world, it is by definition a natural blind spot for us; the complete and total nature its impact on our understanding of everything means we cannot really see how exactly it impacts us. That's why we need another person's help if we want to recognize it, someone that listens to us in a particular way and lets the position become apparent to us.

Ideally this person will be a psychotherapist, someone able to hear beyond the statements of the patient, someone who listens to the place from where their words emerge. This is not always an easy task. Sometimes what a patient tells us is so shocking —as it can be a story of violence, abuse, the suicide of a child— that it is hard to focus on finding the position from where the tragedy is told instead of the tragedy itself, but that will be the way to try to reduce their suffering and to produce some kind of relief, of hope, of the possibility of a future.

This is not to say we should ignore the tragedy or suffering itself all together. All of this listening has to happen without hindering our ability to be empathetic towards the suffering that the statements reflect. Working on those two levels simultaneously is one of the challenges that we face as therapists.

I hope I was able to show this kind of listening in the previous chapters and how, even with interventions at the earliest stages of treatment, it is possible to provoke some changes in the subjective position that will produce relief from symptoms. This, however, doesn't mean that the cases retold here are full psychoanalytic treatments. In fact, they are only the first moves in treatment, something that Lacan would call 'preliminary interviews'.

It's important to highlight this point when we consider the fear many people have of beginning a psychoanalytic treatment, that they assume it will be a long process that will last many years. As the previous chapters show this doesn't have to be the case, a tiny shift in the subjective position — for example ceasing to feel guilty about the death of their partner, confronting the betrayal of their husband, or facing the fears that one has avoided— can provoke in the short term the diminishing, or even end, of the problem that motivated the therapy. Some patients choose to end their work with me after this achievement of their initial goal but this immediate therapeutic effect can also open the door to a path that, if the patient wishes, can be explored further with the help of a psychoanalyst.

I would like to finish this book by sharing a quote by Freud who, in an interview, summed up our work like this: "Psychoanalysis makes life simpler; it gives the thread that allows the person to get out of the labyrinth of their own unconscious."

Acknowledgements

Following a tradition began by Winnicott,
I thank my patients, especially those who were willing
to share their stories, to show that people do change.

This translation would not have been possible
without the help of Peter Gillet, a writer whose prose
I particularly enjoy, and Amy Chapeskie,
a writer and scholar who edited the final version.

My mother, Mariana Rodighiero, checked the book
before its publication and found some mistakes we had
overlooked. For this and for so many other things she
has done for me, I am eternally grateful.

Made in the USA
Las Vegas, NV
29 March 2023

69778230R00069